GET HAPPY TODAY

Your Path to Lifelong Happiness

by

Evelyn Roberts Brooks

Also by Evelyn Roberts Brooks

Nonfiction

Forget Your Troubles: Enjoy Your Life Today

Fiction

The Gypsy Talisman
The Weeping Cameo
The Calico Tapestry

ISBN 978-0-9843781-2-8

www.gethappytoday.com

GET HAPPY TODAY

for Veronica & Carlos
Wishing you a lifetime of happiness together!

Here is my prayer for you:

Dear God, bless our marriage and
help us remember to choose love each morning,
to work out our differences amicably
so we never go to sleep angry, fearful or uncertain.
Please guide us
so we are aligned with your will each day,
to better fulfill our individual purpose in life
and grow together in your love. Amen.

Happiness is like a butterfly which,
when pursued,
is always beyond our grasp,
but,
if you will sit down quietly,
may alight upon you.

~ Nathaniel Hawthorne (1804 – 1864)

Contents

* * *

Introduction

Dear Happiness-Seeker,

Is it really possible to be happy all the time? I know in my heart that it is – because I am.

But it wasn't always that way. I spent far too many years trapped in misery, while smiling on the outside and denying my pain. Nothing I tried made any real difference in how I felt, and I had a sinking feeling that my life was as good as it gets. It seemed like a waste of time to keep wishing for happiness that would never come.

Even though I had achieved outward success and was living extremely well, I wistfully recalled times when I was happier inside and I yearned to recapture that simple joy.

Dissatisfaction and deep unhappiness propelled me to seek the answers. After an extensive process of trial and error, I discovered the secrets of how to be happy no matter what the changing circumstances of my life are.

I believe that we are wired for unlimited happiness. We start smiling as babies but then in the rough scramble to grow up and get ahead, we forget how to be happy.

When you complain that you don't have all the happiness you want, your friends probably tell you to get realistic, to understand life is hard and to stop wanting more. Deep inside you may sense, as I did, that something is fundamentally wrong. You suspect there is a way to feel better, but you don't know how to go about it.

What are you going to do? Take happiness to court? Remain resigned to having a whole lot less than you deserve?

I would like to offer you an alternative. Choose happiness, then feed and nurture it.

Let me share with you the powerful techniques that I have developed over the past fifteen years for creating as much joy as you desire.

I invite you to come on a journey with me and explore the world of inner happiness so that you too can be happy for the rest of your life.

All you need to do is follow the simple instructions in each chapter. Start today to reinvigorate your life. Claim the abundant happiness you've always dreamed of.

Evelyn Roberts Brooks
Los Angeles

Part One

What Stops You from Being Happy?

Chapter 1
Paradise vs. Turmoil

Unlimited joy is your birthright. Happiness is not a matter of chance but rather a deliberate decision combined with the right action taken every day.

Adjust your happiness gauge

Roman Emperor Marcus Aurelius (2nd century A.D.) is credited with saying, "Dig within. Within is the wellspring of good and it is always ready to bubble up, if you just dig."

That advice sounds pretty contemporary, doesn't it? But we usually say: Happiness is an inside job.

An unhappy person can be described in many ways. Here are a few:

- When the possibility of a problem pops up, their mind instantly leaps to the worst case scenario because they are convinced bad things will always happen.

- Even when something great is going on, they hesitate to join in fully because they are waiting for the bottom to fall out.

- If you ask "What's new?" they launch into a long ramble about how bad their life is going.

But an unhappy person can also be someone who has gotten trapped in relationships with people who have a negative outlook, and that attitude has rubbed off on them.

Your perception determines how happy you are. That's the bottom line. No one else can set your level of happiness for you unless you allow them to.

You can even fake it and pretend to be happier than you really are, as I used to do. When you get honest with yourself, as true happiness requires, you will discover, as I did, that dwelling in negative energy is what keeps you unhappy.

It's time to leap onto the "up" escalator to happiness. Claim your rightful destiny, so that you can be everything you want to be. Change the way you view the situations you are in now.

Since you can choose how you see your life, do you see it clearly?

Clarity

What does that word make you think of? A crystal glass, sparkling in the sun?

It probably doesn't make you think of a muddy stream clogged with weeds and fast food wrappers, where you cannot see the bottom. You cannot see the darting fish or the smooth pebbles.

The same is true with your daily life. Getting rid of physical clutter in your home and workplace is a good place to start because you can literally <u>see</u> the difference.

But don't stop there. Go on to unclutter your mind. Stop yourself when you drift into useless thinking and self-recrimination or worry.

Be still. And let life carry you, like you are rafting on a sparkling stream, eagerly taking in the changing scenery.

A popular saying tells us, "Confused minds don't take action." I'll add an observation, "... or they take the <u>wrong</u> action."

By gaining clarity in your life, you rid yourself of the peril of confusion.

When your mind is clogged with regrets for the past and anxiety about the future, you can't live fully in the present. And you can't make informed decisions about what is important to do next in your life.

Discouragement

Ever feel discouraged? I know what that's like. But you don't have to stay down if you don't want to anymore.

If you are feeling discouraged, it means you have lost faith in yourself. You don't have any hope that things will improve.

Here is the general process that your mind might go through:

- I don't like reality! My life should be different!

- I'm afraid I can't handle what is in front of me.

- I feel despair that anything will ever get better. I think the other person should be the one doing the changing.

- Frankly, I don't mean to complain, but this isn't fair!

Have faith that when you change your actions, you will change your feelings.

You've actually got all you need, right now, right here, no matter what. Perhaps you feel skeptical about what I'm saying, but I'll show you how it is true.

You have a purpose for living – right? If you don't, then get one. Think about what you can contribute to the world and then do it.

We are all here for a reason, and we are each going through the exact experiences that we need in order to learn specific lessons about loving one another and ourselves.

It's all about spiritual evolution, baby. Whatever is going on in your life, is there for a reason. Consider it your assignment, and one which you must grasp and complete in your lifetime in order to advance to the next level spiritually.

All of us have different "stuff" happening in our lives. Eckhart Tolle ("The Power of Now") defines it as our life situation and explains that these circumstances are apart from our internal or spiritual life.

Do you think other people have it easier? Given a chance to swap with someone else, you'd probably end up taking your own troubles back, because at least they are familiar. You've got a general idea about what you need to be doing.

Most of the time, though, we don't want to do all the things that seem required. It feels too exhausting. Even when we muddle through and take care of it, the results are not always what we expected.

During rough times, when things aren't going your way, you always have a choice... in how you behave if nothing else.

For some of us, when we are in a state of transient happiness, where life is going smoothly and we are getting what we want in sufficient quantity, we foresee a future with more of the same in it. On those days, we walk with a light step and smile when we hear a bird singing in the trees.

When we are thwarted, however, and when all is not going according to our plan that we've invested so much thought in, then life becomes a tragedy, with only dark clouds in sight and even darker thunderclouds looming on the horizon. Our days are filled with despair and impending doom.

Whether this moment is fulfilling what you think you need, or whether it is presenting a challenge to be met, you still have only this day to live.

Projecting a future where every day from now on will be exactly like this one is a thought process that feels so natural you may think it must be valid. But all it does is become a self-fulfilling prophecy.

If you have an attitude that from now on things will be dismal and hard, then that is what will happen. You will attract the negative into your life. If you have studied the Law of Attraction principles, you are familiar with this concept of like attracting like.

When you attract negative by having a negative view of your world, you will experience life through a filter that sees the mess of the fallen leaves around the tree and the annoying chirp of the song bird. You will not see the beauty and joy.

An alternative is to choose an attitude to adopt each morning, an attitude that says: "I will meet this day head on, and I will take what action is needed to handle what is in front of me in a gracious way, accepting the good with the bad and then letting go when the day is done, to sleep and become refreshed for what the next day will bring."

Take control of your happiness

*"Most people are about as happy as they make up
their minds to be."*

~ Abraham Lincoln (1809 – 1865)

What is happiness? Common answers include bliss, joy, and a sense of satisfaction or contentment with your life.

Does it seem like everybody but you has a say in what your life is like? Your family, your kids, your boss, the neighbors, politicians... the list goes on and on. Maybe it feels like you're a ping pong ball in the game of life, batted back and forth by everyone else, with little say over who whacks you next.

But consider this: If happiness were out of your hands completely, life would be hopeless. And don't you feel at least a glimmer of hope, somewhere deep inside?

Luckily, what President Lincoln said long ago holds true today. An attitude of cheerfulness can direct your thoughts. No, it doesn't mean you'll be slaphappy and grin when another driver rear-ends your car during rush hour.

But if you have a deep wellspring of happiness in your heart, even tragic events cannot wipe you out. You will have an abiding resilience to carry you through the hard times.

How do you get control of your life if everything is a mess and you're overwhelmed? Many times, the struggle for self-control becomes a problem in itself as it gains importance in your mind: "I MUST get control of my life!"

With that thought, your blood pressure rises and your stomach lurches. You feel like a failure, as if you are missing the basic points that everyone else seems to understand.

Maybe you wonder if others were given an "owner's guide" at birth, because they don't have the same troubles you do.

As you wonder what's wrong with you, more stress piles up. What's the solution? Do you abandon yourself to chaos? Let the unpaid bills pile up because you have overspent and perhaps not paid taxes or credit charges on time so that now collection agencies are hounding you?

Do you ignore difficulties so you can play today? Tell everyone defiantly that you are doing the best you can? That you have no choices left? That it's not your fault?

If that kind of thinking is rampant in your mind, <u>stop</u>. Be still for 10 minutes. Breathe quietly. Halt the flood of disjointed thoughts, excuses, worries and anxiety. Calm yourself by breathing slowly and emptying your mind.

As soon as you feel more relaxed and focused, make a list of your difficulties. Formulate a plan for yourself. If needed, get financial advice to get your bills under control. Seek answers to your problems.

When worries threaten to engulf you during the day, remind yourself that you have a plan, and you are working on it. Then do so. Each day, do something towards resolving at least one important item on your list.

You are the Master of your own life. When you abdicate responsibility for yourself, you become a perpetual child. Such a position will lead to feelings of resentment, anger and inferiority.

Instead, you have the choice to take charge, do what you can and get help from others.

Start with stress relief

The buildup of anxiety can lead to even more problems and headaches than you had when you started, because of the exponential growth nature of stress. It doubles and then redoubles the more you ignore your symptoms and keep doing what you've been doing all along.

In some ways, stress is like a cannibalistic monster. It grows engorged, weighing you down as it takes on a life of its own, demanding more and more of your attention.

Stress will eat at you until you are exhausted, yet it still clamors for more: more churning stomach pains, more anguished thoughts, more shot nerves. It thrives on your disease and controls your state of mind so that you cannot feel happy.

Move away from stress-inducing reactions

Let go of <u>desired results</u>. When you already have your mind set on a specific outcome, you are living in the future. And if you are dissatisfied with the present, you probably spend a lot of energy telling yourself things such as, "I can't bear this! I cannot stand another minute of this!"

Solution: Take a deep breath, and make a plan of action. If there's some situation in your life that is a predictable source of stress, plan <u>now</u> to enact a new way of handling things.

Simplify! Group your errands. Build ten- or fifteen-minute breaks into your day so you don't get overwhelmed. Spend less time worrying about what you need to do, and more time taking steps to get things done. You'll feel more in charge.

The more you meekly give in to stress, the more it swallows your life and energy force.

Use this "Moving Away" technique: 1) Stop what you are doing. 2) Physically move away from the problem, even if the only thing you can do is close your eyes softly or turn your head away.

The two-step action can be your private signal to yourself that you are Moving Away from the source of stress, and that you are taking charge of your own feelings and not reacting out of habit. It helps you to step back from the situation and gain perspective.

Release the tension: Push the palms of your hands as hard as you can against a rigid surface such as a tabletop or wall, or even against each other. Breathe slowly and deeply. Feel the physical stress leave your body through your hands.

Try out my quick and effective S.M.A.R.T. system for handling every aspect of your life efficiently and powerfully. You'll find the details in my stress management book, "Forget Your Troubles: Enjoy Your Life Today."

It's hard to be happy and contented with life when your mind is swirling with confusion and anxiety, so do what you need to get that stress level under control.

Here is how to start the process:

- Shrug off disappointments and regret.
- Banish fear, envy, anger and resentments.
- Stop sabotaging yourself.
- Let go of old heartache.

Eliminate wishful thinking

Make a plan of action to deal with your stress in a healthy way through exercise, good food, relaxation and stretching. Engage your mind with other people's lives by helping someone else with their own frustration and confusion.

When you get caught in the trap of wishful thinking, you actually live your life as if you are a child outside the candy store pressing your nose against the glass, longing for what you see but not daring to go in because you think you cannot afford what you want.

Most of the best things in life truly are free: happiness, love, inspiration, friendship. It's a long list and I bet you can add to it with ideas of your own.

Because our society is based on a marketplace economy, it is easy to get caught up in thinking that happiness lies in material goods.

Of course we need a certain amount of the basics: food, clothing and shelter. Beyond that, it's up to individual preferences and financial means.

If you've gotten absorbed in thinking a new "widget" will make you happy, remember that it might make you feel good for a few hours or until the newness wears off, but real joy cannot be bought.

The pattern of chaos

What about that turmoil of yours, that's keeping you from experiencing paradise here on Earth? Do you feel there are too many bad things happening that prevent you from feeling happy?

A sense of overwhelm and anxiety might take over your thinking and push away your satisfaction with life so that you describe yourself as having a really tough time right now. You may feel that you can't possibly be happy until the upheaval settles down.

An important thing to realize is that there will always be ups and downs in life. The more you learn to go with the flow, the easier your time here will be. That's what this book is designed to teach you.

Awareness of how you react to life will help you see where you can change. It's helpful if you look for the pattern first. If you blindly try to apply new thoughts to your behavior, without knowing what the underlying paradigm is, you risk covering up unhealthy thinking patterns that will resurface.

Most people have the same sort of problems and difficulties over and over again. Finding the pattern will help you break free. Until you recognize that there is a template in your life, you will feel like the hapless victim of circumstances.

Take a look at your grocery list. Over a period of time you'll notice the same things crop up on the list again and again. You might always buy long grain rice and orange juice with pulp, while your friend prefers short grain and no pulp.

Those are minor preferences.

We tend to repeat what is familiar. Thus we repeat our lists in other areas of life. For example, you might have the same problem with your boss as with your parents if you have never resolved a dilemma about handling authority issues that troubled you as a teen. Now this dilemma is still in your life because you haven't dealt with it fully.

The opportunity to do so will continue to pop up. That "authority issue" will remain on your list the rest of your life, or until you address it, learn how to handle it and move past the challenge it represents in your emotional and spiritual growth.

Life circumstances can make more sense when you see the common thread. Start noticing how many of the same issues come up again and again. Even after you grasp the lesson, the same thing might pop up to test you, to be sure that you do understand the principles you needed to learn.

You can handle it

Have you ever heard the expression: "You won't get more than you can handle"? Perhaps you bitterly laughed inside, thinking: *"Yeah right, maybe that works for other people but not for me!"*

Guess what? It will indeed work for you, too, but you've probably made the same mistake I used to make all the time.

You see, I never let go of the past, and I also spent a lot of time living in the future by imagining what awful things might happen and how I might handle all the problems. I not only had the "present" to cope with but also all the regrets of things I didn't do right in the past along with worries about the future. What a load to carry each day!

Here's the secret. Imagine you are going through a buffet line. You notice that many people are heaping their plates as high as they can, and also stuffing their pockets and backpacks.

Then you notice someone who only puts on the plate what they can eat in one sitting. You notice that person smiling at everyone, and seeming happy and filled with peace of mind. So, you imitate them.

You take one plateful.

The same thing works in life. Stay in today. Stay in this moment of time.

Catch yourself when you start to worry. Realize that your mind is trying to live in the future. It's physically impossible to do so, but your mind is able to imagine a time that does not exist and never will, since all we ever have is the immediate present.

Learn to think of your day's task load as being a plate of food. Put the most important items on that plate. Don't overload it. Don't fill it with time-wasting fluff that is not nourishing and will leave you unsatisfied.

No fair adding to the plate until it's towering. No fair grabbing from your mate's plate or your child's. Only take the amount you can handle. Take what's yours.

Accept your daily bread. Avoid adding more to your plate from the past and the future.

By strictly limiting your challenges to the present moment, you will not only rid yourself of turmoil but you will find a new sense of calm and order in your life. And you will be able to handle it much more easily.

Chapter 1 – Action Steps: Claim paradise now

1. If you want paradise on Earth, then decide to have an attitude of happiness – it's an inside job and only you can determine how happy you will be. A little bit of happiness or a whole lot? It's your choice.

2. Clarify your purpose in life and avoid feeling discouraged by seeming failures. These are lessons for you to learn.

3. Deal with your stress overload so it doesn't bog you down.

4. Let go of your desired outcome and the results you are hoping for. Eliminate wishful thinking. Concentrate on doing the necessary work in front of you to the best of your ability.

5. Focus on today and this moment in time. Leave the past alone, and stop worrying about your future. You'll be able to handle your life much more easily when you are mentally grounded in the present. Fill your plate with your daily bread only.

Chapter 2

Stumbling Blocks

Let's look at how much you sabotage yourself. How many times in life have you pulled the rug out from under yourself? Where would you be today if you had not burned bridges or made hasty decisions that were not in your own best interest?

Get off your "but's"

Do you frequently respond to life's invitations with a wary, "Yes, that sounds great, but no thanks..." as you continue to stay stuck in less-than-wonderful results and experiences?

Does fear have such a strong grip on you that you feel afraid to move forward but just as afraid to move back to something that felt safe at one time?

When you are trapped by the "but" reaction that prevents you from wholeheartedly embracing life, then you cannot be happy.

These questions are not intended to make you feel bad about yourself. There is not one second of the past that you can change, and it is wasted energy to fret over things you've done up until this moment.

But the reason it is helpful to look at your array of stumbling blocks is that in order to change what you are doing you must first recognize your current behavior regarding your own goals and dreams.

Not the things you "think" you are doing in life, but what you actually are doing, with all the excuses stripped away.

What excuses do you use?

Along with the "yes, but" evasion, your mind has a whole array of excuses that keep you from fully engaging with life at the level your special talents and abilities deserve.

Do you often find yourself making excuses such as:

- I can't.
- I don't know how.
- I am too... (fill in the blank: weak, fat, clumsy, stupid, inept, or whatever limiting label you have for yourself) to do that.

How many times do you make excuses to yourself, and to others, for not participating fully in your own life?

Now, don't think I mean you aren't supposed to ever say "no" to something. Of course you are! But when you have developed a pattern of saying "no" as the easy way out, to protect yourself from risk and from expanding your awareness of others, then it is not a helpful tool.

Think of all the times that you had second thoughts or regrets after you turned down an invitation that seemed too scary when it was first presented to you.

Maybe someone asked you to go camping with them, but your mind instantly filled with fearful thoughts of being out in the wilderness. What if something happened that you couldn't handle or that was uncomfortable? What if you got hurt? What if you got sick far from home?

Instead of taking the chance that things wouldn't be to your liking, you protected yourself and scurried back into your soft cocoon where everything is familiar, predictable and possibly boring.

An excuse is the mind's way to protect you from a perceived danger.

Many times excuses are beneficial, and they work to protect you from making foolish decisions. What if you couldn't say "no thanks" to someone who wanted you to jump out of an airplane without a parachute?

What if you instantly said "yes" to someone who insisted that you put all your savings in their lemonade stand business, with the handshake promise that you'd triple your income overnight?

What if you bought everything that you saw online just because each site had a big red "Buy now" button and you couldn't say "no" to clicking it?

Of course you have to weigh the pros and cons of each situation that comes up in your life, and decide what answer is the right one for you. Accepting invitations doesn't mean you must go white-water rafting if you are a bookworm.

Thrill-seeking is not the same as living fully. Being a risk-taker does not mean you are someone who walks on the railroad track when a train is fast approaching or lives on the edge with drugs and alcohol.

Don't confuse taking risks with being an adrenaline junkie constantly seeking another high to feel alive.

You can be housebound and be more fully alive than that, by developing the quality of your consciousness to a higher level.

The type of excuses that sabotage you are the ones that prevent you from growing and evolving emotionally and spiritually.

Consider the lonely person who is invited to go out with coworkers but always makes an excuse to hurry home after work. Is that a healthy decision, or one that keeps them stuck in a lifestyle that they secretly hate, along with a load of self-contempt for not being able to say "yes" at the right time?

Feeling inadequate

The fear of looking foolish often prevents us from trying new things. We don't want anyone to laugh at us if we fumble or fail in our attempts. So, to be safe, we protect our inadequacies as if they are precious gems. We come up with fancy excuses that secretly defend our right to be stagnant.

If feeling inadequate is an excuse that you recognize, ask yourself about a particular dream you've been avoiding: "What is the worst thing that could happen if I went ahead and tried this?"

Often what our mind grabs onto is the worst case scenario, and it's usually a far cry from the average experience.

Say you've always wanted to go on a TV game show. You watch them all the time, you know how each game works, and you know the answers more often than not. You feel confident that you would be the perfect contestant!

You even find yourself rehearsing clever comments you'd say to the game host when introducing yourself. Perhaps you can hear the appreciate chuckles from the audience.

Then a friend announces that your favorite game show is looking for new contestants and a scout is coming to town next month. You won't have to take time off work or spend money on travel. Maybe they'll pick you for the show.

But what happens? Your mind puts on the brakes! In a panic, you tell your friend that game shows are dumb. They're for lonely people who haven't got anything better to do.

What's going on? ... You're scared!

Suddenly your vision of being the winning contestant with the spotlight on you, is not merely a daydream but something that is going to be put to the test.

And you don't want to risk failure.

So you make excuses. Your heart is pounding and you're dying to say "yes" to being interviewed as a game show contestant. But you can't get your mouth to work. Your head shakes "no" and instead of sticking up for your own best interests, you find yourself saying the word "no" as well.

The game scout comes to town. You don't go to the event. You tell people you are too busy. Maybe you refuse to talk about it. You stop watching game shows, at least for a while.

And then if you do start watching them again, a sour taste comes in your mouth and you find yourself being hypercritical of the contestants, mocking them when they get an answer wrong, telling the TV screen that you knew the right answer and everybody on the show is an idiot.

This can happen even if you are a basically nice and generous person who is quick to praise and compliment other people.

What's happening? Your mind is protecting your ego from pain the best that it can, so that you won't feel bad about sabotaging your chance to have fun on the show and see if you might win.

Instead, what you've got in return for all your excuses and self-sabotage are bitter thoughts and loneliness, and a nagging feeling that this episode of Your Life didn't play out quite right.

Are you tired of doing this kind of thing to yourself?

Let's keep looking at excuses and the damage they do, and then you're going to learn how to turn your stumbling blocks into building blocks.

Bitterness

If you have not fully dealt with and put to rest unpleasant or unhappy events from your past, then each time something new comes up, your mind instantly dredges up the old events to remind you why you should say "no" to this new adventure.

After all, the thinking goes, it was so horrible when you did something similar ten years ago, so why take a chance on repeating that all over again. No thanks!

Even when you realize this is going on in your mind, it can be hard to get past the hurdle. The memory of pain is larger in your head than the perceived joy that might come from the opportunity.

Since it doesn't have a guarantee, it's easy to convince yourself it won't be that great, so why bother spending any time on it.

Result: more self-sabotage.

Disdain

A sense of superiority can often be at the bottom of someone's refusal to join in with fun activities and enjoy their life to the nth degree instead of skating along the surface with minimal joy.

Not that this "superiority" is a conscious thing. It goes hand in hand with emotions such as bitterness and regret, and it's a trick your mind plays to soothe you.

Please note that emotions just "are." They are neither good nor bad. Think of them as arrows expressed in a way to signal your mind about important thoughts and experiences. It's up to you to decipher the meaning of your emotions and see what to do next.

But the problem is, an attitude of disdain for others and their so-called petty activities can keep you aloof from all the conversations, sharing and time together that make up our lives as social animals. The more you feel distant from others, the more you feel disdain to protect yourself from caring... and from hurting.

Nervousness

You know the expression, "Once burned, twice shy"? It means that when you are hurt, you shy away from being hurt again. But some of us keep on trying anyway, with a bright hope that this time things will be different. When we still get hurt, we can eventually reach the point of giving up and saying, "Never again!"

There is a time in life to be sensible. And being afraid of making the same mistake again is a rational fear. But it can – like most good things – be carried too far.

If you have done the emotional footwork to learn why a relationship ended badly, or why you keep being attracted to the same type of person who is all wrong for you, then you are probably at a new plateau. At this stage, you are ready to try something new.

Maybe you've been through counseling or therapy, or you've done a lot of self-reflection and understand yourself better. You want a new relationship that will be healthier this time. You know that it needs to be based on mutual love, trust and respect. You've promised yourself that you won't settle for less.

And yet there you sit, home alone, turning down opportunities to meet new people even though they fit your new set of qualifications. What's going on this time? It's still the same problem: self-sabotage.

Your mind won't let you get past that caution tape – "Do not cross" – because you're afraid that any relationship will result in the same painful process you've already been through time and again.

So you shy away from the dating life, and convince yourself that there isn't anything special about the new people you're meeting. In fact, if you do go out on a date with someone great, you'll do something dumb to make sure it doesn't have a chance of going any further. And you soothe yourself by saying happiness isn't possible anyway.

Nostalgia

Are you caught up in thinking about the "good ol' days"? Do you constantly talk about how much better things were "back then"?

You don't have to be an old-timer to do this. You can be in your twenties and think with longing about high school days and how much greater the guys or gals were then, and how much easier it was to go have fun with your buddies or hang out at the mall.

Life is too hard now, and you've got to keep your nose to the grindstone and take it seriously. But, ahh, those good ol' days. They sure were better than this.

I'm sure you can see the stumbling blocks that this type of nostalgic thinking put in your path. You judge everything according to an imaginary yardstick. You've conveniently forgotten about the real problems you had "back then" and in your memory, everything was perfect!

The past days become your glory days, and nothing you see now can measure up. It's not good enough. You have made the decision to hold the present day in contempt, and not let it engage your full enthusiasm.

What a shame if you let this stumbling block remain. It is one of the biggest hurdles you can face, unless you are willing to let go of the past and realize that the "present" is a gift right in front of you.

Go ahead: open it up and experience the whole array of emotions and lessons it offers.

Don't upset the apple cart

This attitude is one that can subtly sabotage all your projects if you let it. Your thinking might go like this: If I do "that" – the project or trip you yearn for – then "they" will laugh at me.

If you're in a codependent relationship, you risk having your husband or wife ridicule you for trying something new. Or maybe you fear that talking about going back to school to get your degree or a new training will lead to arguments about money. Or you'll have to defend an old dream, and you don't feel you are entitled to it.

You'll learn more about how to let go of these fears, so please keep reading and don't get discouraged.

Unconditional happiness

The bottom line with stumbling blocks is that they prevent you from achieving all that you can in life. You cut yourself off from experiences that enrich and enliven.

When you resist being part of a crowd or a group of friends, when you consistently turn down opportunities that come your way to take an exciting job or move to a new town that you've always talked about, the self-sabotage can take various outward forms.

Some of them sound like this:

- I don't have the time.
- I can't afford it.
- It looks too hard.
- It won't be fun anyway.
- I don't know where to begin.
- I'm too old to change.
- I'll do it as soon as I get a chance.
- But if I start a 4-year course, I'll be too old when I finish it.

For that last excuse, ask yourself: "How old will I be in 4 years if I DON'T pursue this dream?" Guess what? You'll be 4 years older, regardless.

So why not grab that brass ring and fulfill the wishes that you've held in your heart all this time?

Are you tired of missing out on life? Do you want to be really happy, finally?

If your mind and heart are open to experiencing the journey to its fullest, then the task facing you is a fairly simple one: smash those stumbling blocks!

Stop putting conditions on your happiness.

In the next chapter, I'm going to teach you how to BREAK THOSE CHAINS and claim your right to be joyful.

Chapter 2 – Action Steps: Conquer your limiting beliefs

1. Recognize the areas that are stumbling blocks in your life and see your pattern of self-sabotage. Stumbling blocks stay in your way only if you let them. So whether you have to crawl around them, dig under them, or stomp over them, work on removing these obstacles.

2. Feeling inadequate? Break down the task in front of you into manageable chunks and give yourself positive reinforcement at each stage of completion.

3. Bitterness, contempt and disdain can isolate you from the joy of living a full life. Those emotions help you stay distant from other people and inhibit you from starting new projects and relationships. Notice your feelings and take action to move past them.

4. Tackle the fears you have of being hurt again or not having a new relationship live up to the glory of one that is picture-perfect in your memory. Don't let these fears hold you back from experiencing all that life has to offer you.

5. Notice the conditions that you place on your happiness and wellbeing, and consciously challenge the ideas. These limiting beliefs are all in your mind and have little or no basis in fact.

Chapter 3

Break those Chains

Our minds are filled with a never-ending parade of ideas, sensations, words, perceptions and memories.

What's tying you to the past?

It's fine to recognize your past, but don't forget that we exist in the present and that the future is waiting. When you're worried or doubtful about the future, the uncertainties can intimidate you.

We tend to tie ourselves to past events and judge everything else accordingly, comparing every new experience, or every imagined possibility against the past.

You know the person you were then, the exact details of how each event took place, and in what way your concerns were ultimately resolved.

How you bind yourself to your past is of critical significance. It is unhealthy if you are unable to escape from the humiliation, remorse, and hurt from an experience you had, even going back to childhood.

Mistakes you have made should be taken as life's lessons. You can carry each valuable lesson into the present, not by wallowing in your shame and guilt over what you failed to do perfectly, but by learning from what you did and seeing how you could do it differently now.

Be sure not to get into a spin over trying to recreate an incident from the past in your mind so that you can examine it thoroughly. It's easy to get caught up in musing over past episodes to the exclusion of living your life in the present moment. And then you "wake up" one day and realize what month it is, and feel that life is racing by too fast.

The main reason for that sensation is because you spend too much time reflecting about things you wish you could change.

Even if your memories are happy, it is not good to dwell on them too much. Strike a balance between fond memories and staying in the present.

Learn to accept the fact that memories will always remain precious souvenirs of days gone by. What happened in your life before is gone forever and the best thing that can be done about it is to learn.

Research on happiness reveals that happy people tend to be oriented to the present. They live in the "here and now" and let go of the "then and there." That's a helpful motto to take as your own and use to help you stay focused.

Happiness means getting the most out of your everyday life, so focus more on the present. Don't get preoccupied with worries about the future. Release yourself from the nostalgia, regrets and pain of your past.

Mistakes are life lessons

There are no mistakes, but only lessons to be learned. Keep that in mind when you start to scold yourself for making a mistake in a relationship, at work or in an activity that is important to you.

Create positive affirmations that are supportive of our goals. Tell yourself, "I am here to learn important principles about love, spiritual growth, acceptance and wisdom. Although I cannot do everything perfectly, I improve every day in some area of my life!"

When you make a mistake, accept your shortcomings and turn whatever happened into a new opportunity for learning. Consider it a growth opportunity. This attitude will make your life experience more rewarding and will boost your confidence.

Correcting the situation and putting a system in place to prevent the same mistake from happening again is a healthy response.

The worst thing you can do is refuse to notice that you have done something wrong. It is common for people to deny, make excuses, point fingers and rationalize in the face of their own mistakes. However, this only shows that they have not learned to accept the responsibility that comes with their actions.

Three healthy attitudes towards your own mistakes are:

1. Learn the lesson.
2. Move on.
3. Become stronger in the course of action.

Such an approach is a graceful handling of uncomfortable moments that will even enrich your relationship with others. Try it the next time you make a mistake.

Being humans, we will inevitably make mistakes in our lives that we will later regret. All of us can make bad choices or hurt other people's feelings, even inadvertently.

Get in the habit of being aware of yourself and the things you say and do. If you have a pattern of blazing trails everywhere you go, heedless of the consequences, take time to learn the important lessons in life, starting with accountability.

Bear in mind that you are only partly responsible for how others receive you. They may judge you unfairly or harshly despite your best efforts. That's why part of the process involves letting go of what others think of you.

Don't get too caught up in seeking approval from other people or you'll find yourself trapped in the unhealthy "people-pleaser" mode which leads to a lot of stress and unhappiness.

Mistakes are truly life's lessons and by learning from them, you are also developing your own integrity.

Guilt and shame are powerful anchors

Life is inevitably dotted with guilt and shame. These feelings can remain with us long after the incident is over. Memories can torment you time and again if you allow them to control your thoughts and feelings. Regrets, guilt and shame stop you from growing and keep you from being happy.

Solving problems such as marital conflict reduces a lot of unhappiness in your life. In the same way, working through the blemish of an abusive childhood frees your mind of emotional baggage. Liberating yourself from a deep-seated fear or insecurity can also make your life easier.

This is not enough, though, because unhappy memories can build up over the years and damage your health. Trapped emotions create internal strain which can result in psychological and physical problems.

You can't please everyone

Happiness follows naturally when you are comfortable with yourself. People who are spontaneous, unaffected and candid are more likely to be happy than those who suppress their authentic self and worry constantly about what others think of them.

The desire to live up to everyone's expectations is a flawed attempt to fit in and be accepted by family and friends. And since you can't please everyone, this attitude often creates a deep well of unhappiness that sours even the occasions that should be happy ones.

Allowing other people's expectations of you to rule your actions will end up in nobody being pleased. Most especially yourself! Nobody can meet the competing expectations of parents, friends, coworkers or boss and the community at large.

The outcome could be to make yourself miserable because you will be living a life that you don't want in the first place.

Sometimes well-meaning parents or other relatives label a family member as being a certain personality type or inadequate for some kinds of work. Limiting beliefs were discussed in "Chapter 2, Stumbling Blocks" and it's important to recognize if you've been pigeonholed.

Friends may give advice based on an incorrect assessment of who you really are. Be cautious about buying into the opinions others have if they don't accurately describe what you want to achieve. You don't have to completely ignore their advice but it is important that you are not afraid of what they think when you strike out on your own path.

You are the only one who knows yourself well. Having the initiative to realize your potential and changing unwanted habits largely depends on you.

The basic traits of a happy personality include feeling good about yourself. You have to like who and what you are as a person, and accept yourself. Become comfortable with your shortcomings and limitations while you work on improving yourself and striving for spiritual growth.

Happy people are honest with themselves. They are able to trust themselves, are self-reliant, independent, motivated and are comfortable with their place in society. They don't feel an urgent need to please everyone at the risk of failing to be true to themselves and their higher calling.

Happiness goals

If you can't describe yourself as a happy person yet, then think of these attributes as goals to work toward. When you have specific traits that you want to achieve, it becomes easier to keep moving forward and practice "acting as if" you already have those traits.

For example, if you want to feel more comfortable at parties, practice saying to yourself, "I am at ease in my own skin. I am happy with who I am."

When you get to the party, go with the attitude of being centered in your own spirit. Instead of worrying what others will think about what you're wearing or how your hair looks... and instead of worrying what you will say or who you will talk to... break that shyness and insecurity chain by giving yourself an assignment: that you will make other people feel more comfortable.

That's your job for this party. Go up to someone who is standing alone or looking shy, and strike up a conversation by asking how they know the party host, or talk about the food being served.

Get out of yourself by putting the focus on the other person and their desire to feel liked and secure. This technique works to help you stop being self-conscious. Give it a test-run the next time you are in a new setting and feel uncomfortable.

Stop worrying what others will think

When you are secure in yourself, you stop worrying what others will think about you.

It is understandable that you care about other people's opinions but it should not be to the extent that their judgments become the guide post in your life, instead of your own goals.

People who are physically, emotionally and mentally healthy attain a sense of internal balance. This makes it easier for them to trust their own decisions. It is your intuition as well as the direction that your heart wants to take you, that should dictate your actions.

The way most people respond to your actions is not really about you. In most cases, it is about them. Unfortunately, because of the differences between people, not everyone is going to like you or approve of you and your lifestyle.

You will find it easier to be happy when you view the differences and diversity of humankind as interesting. When someone does not think highly of you, it does not necessarily mean there is something wrong with either of you. More likely, you are on different wavelengths.

The danger of trying too hard to please others is that you may end up compromising your values and opinions.

Constantly trying to make people like you and worrying about what they think of you can lead you to have an artificial personality. You may get sidetracked by pretending to be something you are not.

The result is that you have strained relationships with other people because you must keep up the pretense of agreeing with them even when you have a growing resentment about the situation.

Your intuition that something is wrong can be the signal that you need to start getting honest with yourself, first of all, and then with others.

Debunk the myth that serious means unhappy

Having a serious character has been known to characterize unhappy persons. This is certainly not true because happiness is a state of mind. It is not a reaction to a particular person, thing, or event.

Real joy is when you can be happy no matter what happens to you. In the same vein, you can be happy whether you are married, widowed, divorced or single. As long as you are alive, you can make yourself happy.

Happiness is part of a special category of emotions that includes joy, pleasure, satisfaction and contentment.

In many cases, people pretend to be "fine" to please their family or friends even though they are depressed or deeply troubled. The stress of presenting a false face adds to the burden of pain. This person is headed for a breakdown unless they get help.

All that we need in life is a handful of people that truly accept us for what we are. Some people put on a cheery front to become popular and admired by others. But there are also those would trade all that for a few good friends who really like them.

Friends accept us the way we are, whether we have a lively personality or a serious nature. It is more crucial to be natural and be yourself.

Break free for your soul's sake

A lot of people never venture beyond their comfort levels. They spend most of their lives maintaining an existence and defending just that.

Others want more out of life. They actively pursue happiness, realizing it is the most important thing in their lives. Aside from being true to yourself and focusing on the present, there are many ways of achieving bliss and contentment.

An active and rewarding social life has a major effect on personal happiness that is far more important than business success, income and partying.

You can achieve happiness by having a life of continued growth and finding purpose through your work or profession. The most obviously harmful thing in the pursuit of happiness is worrying. Most of the time, people worry over trivial things.

Teaching yourself to have low levels of anxiety will make you a happier person, just as positive thinking will have a strong influence on your own personal happiness level.

The ability to view situations in a positive light makes any difficulty feel more manageable instead of overwhelming.

It's not that happy people have fewer personal problems. The difference is that they learn how to discipline themselves to control their fears, hostilities and anxieties. And you can learn this same discipline.

Chapter 3 – Action Steps: Claim your joy now

1. When a survey asked, "What is the most important thing in life?" the majority of the people answered, "Happiness." Decide now if you want happiness enough to pursue it.

2. True abiding happiness is an overall sense of personal well-being and contentment with life, and you can learn to recognize it and cultivate it on a daily basis.

3. You are entitled to happiness, be it fleeting or sustained. Drop any guilt feelings that being <u>unhappy</u> demonstrates responsibility. That's a myth.

4. Build your happiness level by seeking joy and pleasure in the small everyday things around you. A child's laugh, a sunny day, a quiet chat with a dear friend. Take time to notice the beauty that is in your life.

5. Break free from the expectations of society and find happiness to enrich your soul in a simpler lifestyle rather than feeling you "must" have certain material things to be happy.

Chapter 4

Your Dream Life

How can you figure out what your best life would be? And then how you can stack the odds in your favor?

Dream about it! Know that your life can be as happy and fulfilling as you desire, but you must be specific in what you wish for.

Mind-map your ideal life

Give yourself the opportunity to explore and daydream about the kind of life that is most meaningful to you. You'll never be truly happy and contented with your life unless it has a purpose that resonates deep within you.

You may know of people who chose a career and lifestyle based on their family's expectations or on seeking wealth. They told themselves it didn't matter whether this was what they wanted, because money would bring happiness eventually.

If you feel unhappy about the life you are now leading, it's not too late to shift gears.

If you've gotten off track with a job that you hate or an expensive lifestyle that causes more worries than pleasure, look at the facts and see what changes you can start making today.

You might not have to do anything more radical than downsize to a simpler, more affordable home or apartment. Or stop chasing that next big promotion when you realize that you don't even want it. You may be caught in a success mindset that pushes you to grab more and more each year to avoid feeling like a failure.

When you mind-map your dream life, you treat it as you would your most important project at work. Remind yourself that your life is worth living well, and then write about your goals and intentions. Think where you want to be in five years, ten, fifteen and more. And visualize the steps it will take to get there.

Map it out for yourself in broad strokes, so you can recognize the journey ahead. This will help you stay on course when you are tempted to stray into old patterns.

Seek lasting treasures, not temporary pleasures

Pleasure-seekers make a career of chasing physical pleasures and transient joys. They live for the moment rather than "in" the moment. They don't do this in a healthy spiritual way of trusting their creator and not fearing the future, but rather in blind seeking of sensual numbness and thrills to stave off their fears of getting old.

This type of person is not a good companion for the true seeker of life wisdom and happiness. Think of them as being like empty shells. There is little substance to them.

The danger is that the seeming fun and liveliness they have can draw you into their world of emptiness.

Warning: it's a diet made of spun sugar. It won't sustain your spirit. It can be fine for a diversion but it's not meant to be the meal of your life, not if you want to survive and grow emotionally and spiritually, which I believe is our purpose for being here in this physical world.

Look at their eyes, and look at their moods. You will probably find a lack of connection with life because of the shallow nature of their pursuits.

Understand the difference between enjoying life and seeking constant pleasure.

Pursuit of happiness refers to going after the depths of life and spiritual contentment. It doesn't mean you must take on the lifestyle of a monk, but be aware that when you are feeling unhappy, that void inside will not be filled by another shopping spree or late night of drinking and partying.

The true treasures of life consist of intangible things such as:

- A loving family.

- Deep, abiding, interdependent love for your life partner.

- Close-knit friendships.

- Sustaining belief in a higher power (God, Universal Love, Great Spirit).

- Passion for your life's work.

- Joy in using your special talents to help others.

- Lasting pleasure in the beauty of nature.

- Knowledge that you are using your time well, to love others and grow.

Do what you love daily

A lot of people believe that they will be happy when they become successful, but as soon as they achieve one level of success, they are dissatisfied and seek to go even higher, thus putting another condition on happiness that keeps it out of their reach.

The luckiest people discover ways to spend their talent doing what they love to do. Someone might judge from the outside that the job is not lofty enough, and yet if the person feels fulfilled and useful, it doesn't matter whether the person is a street sweeper or a board room executive.

Find ways to bring your own personal touch to your work. If you are in a large office, you can spread cheer and goodwill. Maintain an attitude that the work you are doing is meaningful to the company and its customers. You are an important and vital part of the flow of energy.

Since happiness is a personal decision, it does not depend on what is going on around you. When you decide to love what you are doing, you will notice opportunities to feel successful throughout each day.

When you are excited about what you do, it will not feel like hard work. You'll engage yourself fully in the tasks and feel good about your accomplishments.

Understand that you have the power to shift your attitude so that you find peace of mind and satisfaction in your work, no matter what it is.

Focus on your dreams each day

It's easy to lose focus in life and get caught up in all the daily dramas. You may feel tired at the end of the day when you have put your energy into activities that are mentally draining or that you resist because it's not your top choice of work.

You may feel that it's better to put off doing what you want because it's not practical, or because it would require a big commitment of time and energy that you fear others would criticize.

This attitude can sneak up on you as you gradually spend more and more time working hard to maintain a lifestyle that you might not even find fulfilling.

Many people end up trapped and so they abandon their personal dreams and try to convince themselves that it doesn't matter.

Telling yourself that what you want is not important, or that it's a wish left over from childhood, won't trick your heart and soul into giving up the dream. What happens instead is that you feel cheated and resentful.

You may start noticing that a friend who pursued his dream is now enjoying success that you don't have. Instead of taking that as inspiration to go back to your own dream life, you may get caught up in envy and other self-defeating reactions.

The feelings of bitterness will age you quickly and push away your chance of achieving happiness. We talked about bitterness in "Chapter 2, Stumbling Blocks" because it blocks you from feeling happy and contented.

You should realize that pursuing your dream life requires learning to value yourself.

When you come to a decision that your life is worth the effort, and then keep on going despite obstacles, life will cast opposition along the way. Consider these obstacles as tests to see if you have what it takes to achieve. Only the strong survive.

What kind of "tests" might they be? They come in many forms such as a new relationship, a new passion, or the lure of hobbies and major projects in your profession.

It is easy to get sidetracked and pour your heart into something that is not truly important to you, only because in a hasty moment you agreed to the task or project.

Consciously and unconsciously, we tend let go of our dreams far too easily.

To focus on your dreams each day, make them concrete. If you write it down on paper, it becomes more tangible. State your goals in a positive way so they are inspiring and simpler to focus on. Making your goals objectively measurable will help you see your progress. Saying your dream aloud will make it vivid.

Visualize yourself leading your dream life. This will keep you motivated and focused.

By following these steps, it becomes easier to see if you've drifted off course. If so, you can take action to get back on track with your dream.

Cure boredom and dissatisfaction

When you are discouraged about reaching your goals, boredom and dissatisfaction can set in. You may lose interest in what you are doing. It might feel too hard and not worth continuing. You may find yourself in a state of being restless and tired.

Anxiety comes when you feel that the demands of your dream are more than your abilities, while boredom arises when the task is not stimulating enough. Monotony is one aspect of boredom. Your attention fades when you are exposed to constant repetition.

When someone asks how you're doing, you might reply, "Oh, you know, same old same old." You can become disconnected from your goals when your mind is running on automatic.

Solution? Design your daily activities with variety to make life more interesting. Being bored is a condition of passivity. Shift into a more active attitude of thought and behavior. Remind yourself that you are going to fulfill your dream but you must be patient.

Enjoy the different stages along the way where you've achieved a new level of accomplishment. This will help you take charge of your life and adopt a helpful attitude of enthusiasm, interest and personal commitment towards the things that you do.

Take a break and assess if what you are doing is what you truly love. Are you getting nearer to the realization of your dream? Or are you using procrastination as an excuse to avoid moving on to the next, more challenging, stage of your dream life? Refer to your mind-mapping goals frequently so you can keep yourself on track.

Live actively

A big part of achieving goals and dreams is having enough physical energy to pursue them.

If you're not sure where to start to have a more active life, take a look at all the ways you can be more physical. Where possible, walk or ride a bike instead of driving your car. Take the stairs rather than the escalator or elevator. Jog in place while you're waiting for the microwave to ding.

Do simple stretches throughout the day, especially when you've been sitting for a long time at the computer or watching TV. At least three times a week, opt to do more strenuous exercise like dancing (put on music and dance by yourself – it's fun and it's free), running, power-walking, lifting hand weights (for a lightweight workout, use canned food from your pantry if you don't own dumbbells), going to the gym, swimming, or playing a sport.

People who increase their physical activity also tend to improve their diet, even if they hadn't intended to do so at first. As you move around more and enjoy feeling fit, you'll naturally choose fruit over candy, and light salad dressings over a rich creamy type.

Healthier food choices help you to reach and maintain your ideal weight and also reduce the risk of chronic life-shortening conditions like heart disease, cancer and diabetes.

A more fit and healthy life will have a positive impact on your mood. People who join wellness programs improve their job performance and morale, and are more likely to achieve their goals and dreams.

Avoid passive resignation

If you are dissatisfied with the current state of your life, start making some positive changes and in the process, make your life better. Realize that you create your own reality to a great extent.

When you lose initiative and become resigned to the way things are, you lose motivation for change. You've probably heard friends talk with resentment about their lives and all the bad breaks they've had, as if there is nothing they can do about it. That is passive resignation.

It can be easy to slide into the conversation and become a complainer as well. Instead, reverse that trend by becoming a "doer" in life. Make a difference for yourself and others by getting busy with projects that are significant and helpful.

Are you passive about your dream life? If you're not sure whether you are or not, ask yourself if you want to do something but you never muster the courage to do it.

Feeling overwhelmed and stressed can lead to feeling bored with your life. You lose your old enthusiasm to do things you used to enjoy. Everything you think of sounds like too much effort.

Set short term goals. Don't put off projects out of procrastination, mental fatigue or laziness. When you are able to accomplish small things such as taking care of the household chores as needed, then you gain confidence for your bigger dreams and goals in life.

Generate compassion

Compassion involves a warm heart, serving other people, helping others, respecting others and being less selfish. By showing compassion, you can achieve long lasting inner happiness, and your everyday life will feel more useful and meaningful.

Researchers have shown that there are physical, emotional and spiritual benefits in being compassionate. However, the biggest benefit of all is that practicing compassion makes people happy.

Make compassion a priority in your life and see the difference it makes.

Cultivating compassion and using it every day is an important happiness tool. It's okay if you start off doing it simply for the benefit. Gradually you will incorporate empathy into your heart more and more. Compassionate feelings will flow naturally from you instead of feeling forced or artificial.

Although most people believe they have empathy, too often they are centered on themselves and their own concerns.

If you feel your sense of empathy has grown rusty, practice listening to your family members and friends. Ask questions about how they are and how their life is going. Show your interest and offer supportive comments.

Avoid the tendency to judge or tell them what they need to do to correct their mistakes. Be a friendly listener who is on their side.

You might say something to them such as, "It sounds like you are going through a rough time right now. I'm glad we were able to talk and I hope you know you can count on me because I care about you." That's empathy!

Notice that you're not jumping in to solve problems for them. They need to solve their own problems if they are going to be the master of their life and grow emotionally as well as spiritually.

Instead, you offer a listening ear and a compassionate heart. You engage with them about what is important but you remain positive and encouraging. Generate compassion by experiencing the other person's emotions from their point of view.

Put yourself in the shoes of those who suffer so that you will feel a genuine compassion for their plight. And in order to alleviate such suffering, try to do some kindness. It could come in the form of a smile, a kind word, doing an errand or chore, or talking about possible solutions for their problems.

Create harmony around you

The desire for harmony will help you achieve your dreams and goals.

Realize that the force of life is present inside us and in all the things around us. This energy is what sustains the whole universe.

To produce harmony around you, start by erasing ugly thoughts from your mind and heart. Believe that perfection, balance, beauty and harmony is in everyone to some degree despite outward appearances.   As you pursue your dream life, remember to treasure the lessons of the past and dream about the future but live each day on its own merit.

Chapter 4 – Action Steps: Turn your dream life into a reality

1. Reorganize your time so it does not enslave you. A balanced rhythm of activities gives you the freedom to engage with your dreams.

2. Follow a daily exercise regimen that permits a free flowing movement of your body while you allow your thoughts to reflect on the details of your dream life.

3. Simplify your life. Get rid of unnecessary chores, phone calls, email and errands. Streamline your schedule as much as you can so there is room for your fabulous new dream life to come into being.

4. Practice positive thinking and think well of the people around you instead of criticizing them.

5. Create harmony around you as you go through life with a smile, choosing compassion as your priority and refusing to give up when you have setbacks.

Chapter 5

Grateful Heart

Does leading a life of contentment sound impossible, or something only for a few lucky folks? Actually, it is a process that is teachable. If you diligently follow the simple steps in the process, you can learn it, too.

It's more a matter of making a commitment to yourself than it is hard work.

Achieve lasting peace of mind

Once you remove the mystique and the aura around phrases such as "peace of mind," "happy all the time" and "easy in your own skin" you realize these things are all natural to human beings but we've forgotten our primary spiritual connection.

In the rush and crush of daily living and keeping it all together, who has time to think great thoughts or study philosophy? You might buy a few books or bookmark some web sites that look intriguing, but then you get busy and neglect to read them.

The problem with ignoring your spiritual needs is that it affects your entire outlook on life and whether or not you feel satisfied with your accomplishments and growth.

You've got one, we've all got one

Whether you believe in a certain religion's tenets, or disdain anything and anyone who tells you what to think about matters of the soul, every one of us is a spiritual being.

Each individual has a soul, or spirit.

We are not robots stomping through life until our metal parts wear out and we topple over to rust away.

Although some people you meet might remind you of an automaton, even the most difficult, hard-nosed person you come across is a spiritual being at the center of the all-too-human flaws they flaunt.

Do you know people you might describe as soul-less? Their behavior is nasty and self-absorbed. If you can avoid this person, do so, because their negative energy will suck you dry.

Say a prayer for them if you are so inclined and then stay away as much as possible. When you do have to be around them, be on guard against adopting their negative ways.

Happiness is an inside job

When someone in your circle of family, friends and coworkers is in a dark place and is focused on selfish matters, you cannot help them no matter how much you try to be a good example or point out the error of their thinking.

These efforts may be well-intentioned, but they are generally not well-received by the other person and will only serve to get you stuck on a merry-go-round of believing you are somehow responsible for "making" them happy. You're not.

Everyone, including you, is responsible for their own emotional state.

We often use "heart" and "soul" together, because we have come to see the heart as our center of love. And your spirit/soul is all about love, or the lack of it.

From now on, do your best to surround yourself with people who are loving, kind and happy.

Hang out with happy people! Not only will their mood rub off on you, but together you will build a synergy of happiness that will spread like wildfire.

Make gratitude your attitude

A quick way to feel better and more centered in your spirit of love is to think of something you are grateful for. This can be anything from being happy and grateful to be alive to grateful for your new pair of shoes.

Focus on gratitude, and your other issues will become more manageable.

Get your life in perspective and don't put too much emphasis on things that go wrong. Instead, take a look at all that is going right! I think you'll find the list is a long one, but maybe you've become complacent about noticing the good things in your life.

When you first start making a grateful list, you might not even know where to start. It doesn't matter. There are no right or wrong lists.

It is all personal and unique to the individual, so don't worry about competing with someone else's "perfect list" – there is no such thing. One person might put that they are grateful for the squirrels in their backyard, and another might be grateful that their favorite sport team won the big game last night.

Your "Grateful Journal"

If you start a Grateful Journal you can watch the progression of where you find gratitude. Simply jot down today's date and put a few bullet points. No need to write long sentences unless you wish to.

What a grateful list does for you is remind you of all the blessings that you have around you every single day. In a hectic life, it can be easy to get caught up in the drama of financial goals or wanting a new car, new clothes, new things.

I remember the first time I learned about making a grateful list, many years back, and I was nonplused. All I could think of was being grateful for material things – food in the cupboard, clothes on my back, a place to live. Of course those are something to be grateful for, but it took a while for me to expand my gratitude to include intangibles.

Be easy on yourself with this task. If you find it a challenge, start with the first letter of the alphabet and write about anything that starts with "A" that you feel grateful for. Tomorrow, use "B" and so on. The alphabet approach helps jump start your grateful process.

If your mind is blank, start off by looking around. Are you wearing shoes? Can you find gratitude in your heart for the fact that you don't have to trudge through life barefooted, picking up thorns and cuts?

A friend of mine who takes yoga classes related that one day the instructor said, "If you have a yoga mat and clean water, be grateful. You have more than many people in the world."

It's easy to overlook the abundance in your life. Complacency slips in and all you notice is what you don't have and wish you did. Take a moment to pay attention to the lifestyle you lead, and be grateful for it.

Since this is not meant to be an exhaustive list, but rather a practice to help you focus on your blessings, limit your list to three to five items each day.

Throughout the day, pause now and then and think of your list. It's okay to add more things to it mentally as you go about your day.

Thanking others

A side effect of writing a gratitude list is that you will gradually find yourself more grateful for the people in your life.

Go ahead and express your gratitude to them! See what a difference it makes. Not only will they be pleased (possibly startled) but you will feel love expanding inside you.

If you're at work and someone helps you with a productivity tip that resolves a problem, tell them, "Thanks so much! I'm grateful for the help." Letting the other person know you are grateful for them helps both of you grow.

Take a few moments each day to become aware of all that you have. This opens the door onto new spiritual and emotional growth you might have been missing. Gratitude plays into the Law of Attraction and you will see that the more you are grateful for positive things in your life, the more positive things show up.

You can't do both

Both what? It's impossible to be both grateful and hateful at the same time.

Go ahead. I'll wait while you try it. Think of someone you dislike, or who irks you. Now find some reason to be grateful they are in your life circle.

At first, your gratitude might be grudging. Let's say you had to take your car back to the dealership for a repair, and the service guy is one you've talked to before. He rubs you the wrong way with a false friendliness, but he's good at his job. So you might say to yourself, "Well, he's a pompous ass and I can't stand him, but I'm grateful that he helped me today."

You may have noticed that in the examples given thus far, you are being grateful for something good that the other person does for you. Later in this chapter, I'll show you how to be grateful even when someone behaves badly.

Butterflies, orchids and starry nights

Here's another quick tip for grabbing a grateful attitude: get out in nature and enjoy the awe-inspiring beauty of flowers, butterflies, birds and other critters.

If you can, keep living plants around you, even if it is merely a potted plant on your desktop or kitchen counter. Also, if possible, put outside your window a bird feeder filled with seeds or a hummingbird feeder filled with nectar.

Once you start feeding the birds, be sure to make a commitment to keeping their feeder clean and full of fresh food, because they will start to rely on it. One caution: if you use bird seed, be sure to clean up the ground below it or you will attract rodents who eat the seeds the birds scatter.

For those who do not have access to a garden or yard, that's no reason to skip this process. Here are solutions for you:

- Browse your local flower shop, enjoying the lovely blossoms.

- Take a day trip to a nearby botanic garden or city park.

- Go online and check out the web sites for seed catalogues and nurseries. Take 10 minutes for a virtual nature walk.

- Check out nature books and videos at your local library.

- Watch nature shows on TV.

- Go outside after dark and star-gaze. This can be a challenge for people in big cities, but you should at least be able to see the moon and a few stars. Look northward and try to find the Big Dipper, if you are in N. America – it is usually visible even when other constellations are diminished by light pollution.

- If you can get near a body of water such as an ocean, lake or river, sit calmly and watch the tide or flow of water. Reflect on the fact that you, too, have an ebb and flow of days in your own life.

- Make yourself part of the world's picture and understand that you are a spectacular creation of nature as much as the flowers and birds are.

Learn how to be grateful for the wonderful world we live in and all its beauty. In the next chapter, I'll teach you how to grab a cheerful outlook and make it your own, but let's keep talking about how you can incorporate a grateful heart into your life and use it to help you cope.

Courage

As you learn to be grateful for the bounty in your life, realize there is so much more to living than the daily process of getting up and going to work or taking care of the home.

You are on a spiritual journey, one which many people believe you planned before birth because there were specific lessons that you wanted to concentrate on in this lifetime.

Whether you believe such a pre-planning is possible is not the point. Stop and think about the concept of learning something special. It might be how to be more generous, how to be a better listener, how to be more patient and kind.

Where are you in the lesson plan? What have you learned so far? Do you have the courage to keep going and learn even more?

A saying that you may find helpful is: "Courage is fear that has said its prayers."

Someone who acts with bravery is not fearless. They have learned how to ACT anyway, in spite of being fearful. You can do this too, no matter what challenges face you.

Are you willing to do that? If so, repeat this to yourself, "I have the courage to claim happiness, from now on, no matter what!"

Be thankful for others in your life

Consider that you are on a journey. It usually starts and ends with different people around you. Not everyone you know will be with you for the entire length of your journey here, but you have the opportunity to meet so many special individuals who will help you along in life, and you can help them in return.

Think of vacations you've taken, where you might spend an amazing time with great people you encounter and yet you understand at the end of the vacation you'll say goodbye. You enjoy knowing them, and perhaps even promise to keep in touch, but you accept the brief nature of the relationship.

Life is the same, but we generally have more than two weeks to get to know and interact with the people around us. Take advantage of all the chances you have to interconnect with others. We all learn and grow from these links and experiences.

Now that you've had a taste of being grateful for material goods, your general welfare and the beauty of nature, stretch yourself to find something – even one small thing – to praise in every single person that you meet.

How is that possible? Look on all you see as being a unique creation that has merit. If you've only been judging appearances, delve deeper. Find something to compliment or thank the universe for.

Notice in the following examples that there are times you will be grateful for someone's behavior because they are pointing out how <u>not</u> to act in life. Don't get derailed by the idea that you must find something praiseworthy in negative or abusive behavior.

What you may find, as you become a student of humanity, are countless demonstrations of attitudes and actions that you will now consciously avoid because you can see the repercussions. Thank that person in your mind for giving you a free lesson. You can avoid the mistakes they make, instead of having to repeat them in your own life.

All of us are teachers, you see, but some people teach us what <u>not</u> to do!

See what lessons these three people might teach you:

- You meet a woman who is loud-mouthed, bitter and disgruntled. Instead of being put off by her outward "self" you take a moment to say hello in a kind voice, and ask how her day is going. If she rattles off complaints, politely interrupt and ask if she has any pets. Often the mere mention of their pet cat, dog, bird, fish or small furry friend like a hamster or ferret, will break through the self-centered tirade. The woman smiles. She admits that she has a pet rat – a white rat that sits on her shoulder while she watches TV. Ask how she came to have such an unusual pet. Take a few moments out of your life to engage with this stranger in a compassionate way. Be thankful she gave you a free lesson in the joy of having a pet. She's also given you a lesson in the unpleasantness of being a complainer: so take that lesson to heart and don't do as she does.

- A man at work stops by your desk and tries to get you to chat. He's so boring that you automatically mutter about a crucial deadline, lower your head and get busy with your computer or telephone. He shuffles off, rejected. Today, however, do something different. Before he gets started on his rounds, seek him out at his work station. Pause for a moment, say hello cheerfully and wish him a great day. Then move on. It might help to mentally play the role of a person you admire such as Mother Teresa or Nelson Mandela. Copy the way they passed through a crowd, smiling benevolently on each person. And meanwhile, learn a lesson from your coworker: everyone craves human contact, and you can be part of the love chain. Mentally thank him for the opportunity to be a conduit of love.

- Your spouse or another family member slams into the kitchen and does not even greet you. This happens all the time. Your usual mode is to make an arch comment such as, "Well it looks like someone had a bad day today!" But tonight, unh-uh. The old pattern has you stuck in feeling superior and that is not a loving position. So what lesson can you learn that involves gratitude? How about, "Hey there, I'm so glad you're home. Let's fix something to eat. Or would you rather call for takeout?" Be thankful this person, even though they are demonstrating grumpiness at this moment, is part of your circle. Imagine life without them. Even if there has been strife between you, you can probably dredge up memories of good times. What's stopping you from gently offering a hug and a kind word?

A trip to the dentist became a grateful lesson

While writing this book, I had to go to the dentist for what I thought would be a minor procedure. Instead, he said he'd have to perform surgery right then to correct an allergic reaction I was having to the prior dental work. I ended up in the chair for two hours, when I thought I'd be there ten minutes.

My mind instantly filled with frantic thoughts about the expense, the pain of the injections he'd be giving me to numb the area, the recovery time, etc.

But since I am your happiness guru, I knew it was a danger zone to stay in the FEAR and so I immediately shifted into slow, deep breathing.

I mentally sought something to cheer myself up and these words came to me: *"Don't be fearful, be cheerful!"* I couldn't recall ever hearing that before, and decided it was a great new saying that I'd pass along. I gave thanks for the inspiration, feeling that the words came to me at the moment I needed them.

I reminded myself that a helpful use of the acronym FEAR is one that I created for myself because most of the ones I've heard create negative images.

FEAR = "Face Each Anxiety Realistically." When you stop your imagination from going wild in a blind panic, you can get on track with a more reality-based and rational approach to the situation in front of you.

While I looked out the window at treetops and clouds, I told myself: "Quick! Find something to be grateful for."

I knew that if I stayed in the fear, the whole experience in the dental chair would be even worse, so I pushed myself to focus on gratitude... and began giving myself mental messages while waiting for the dentist to come back in the room and start the procedure. Here is what I told myself:

"I am grateful my dentist is so good that he recognized the allergic reaction and knows how to fix it. I am grateful I have a credit card that I can use today if there is an extra charge. I am grateful that he will give me injections to numb my mouth during the procedure because many people alive today – let alone humans throughout history – have to endure surgeries with no anaesthesia or novocaine. I am grateful that it's not worse. He didn't say that I've got cancer of the jaw and they must remove half of my face. That does happen to people. I am grateful to be here, right now."

The reason I've shared with you the step-by-step thought process I went through is so that you can see how simple it is, and you can adapt it to your own life as needed.

Chapter 5 – Action Steps: Cultivate gratitude

1. Don't expect yourself to be a magical mystical being who doesn't have fear and who dances through life with a song on your lips every moment of every day. That's not what being "happy no matter what" means. Happiness is an intention to accept the ups and downs with good humor.

2. Be grateful for every chance to love someone who is, at this point in time, acting in an unlovable way. Isn't that what love is all about?

3. There's no mystery to how I went quickly from panic to acceptance in the dentist chair. But there is indeed a secret that I will share with you, and here it is: I used gratitude as my path.

4. Make gratitude a habit in your daily life. It works.

5. From now on, in everything you do, even the mundane tasks, find ways to say to yourself, "I am grateful for this situation because..." Try it. With practice, it leads you to feel more empowered about your life. As well as happier.

Chapter 6

Don't Worry, Be Happy

Can worrying too much and too often actually destroy you?

Worry is toxic

It affects your stress level, which in turn affects your health in negative ways.

Many people feel that excess worry can be self-predicting, in that you affect the outcome of your life situations because of all your anxiety.

Friendships and romances fall apart because the people around you get tired of hearing every detail of your constant drama. You're no fun to be around with all that complaining! But what if you're not the one instigating the dramas?

You can still get sandbagged by the worry habit.

Imagine a scenario where you excitedly tell a close friend all about your new romantic relationship and how happy you are now. For whatever reason – their own unhappiness, envy, a self-righteous decision to make sure you remain available to them instead of overly involved with your new love – the close friend sets about a systematic program to undermine your new love relationship.

This is not something they are consciously deciding to do, and in fact they probably feel justified in "helping" you to see the light.

They start off by warning you sadly that your new relationship is not going to last. They are only telling you this for your own good because you are too infatuated to see the facts. This preliminary salvo is followed by a steady assault of critical comments about your new love.

At first, you resist. But as they continue bad-mouthing your boyfriend or girlfriend, pointing out every flaw in your partner and heaping on remarks that are all about failure, gradually you start having fights with your new mate. Maybe your "close friend" has insinuated ideas into your mind that your mate is unfaithful or is looking around for other dates on the sly.

This seed of worry grows into jealousy and soon you start accusing your mate of wanting to leave. You refuse to believe their protests. You run to your close friend and pour out your feelings of panic that the relationship is crumbling.

Day by day, the poison that your toxic friend has dripped into your mind changes the way you act around your new love. You watch him or her suspiciously. You make subtle remarks that reveal your unhappiness. You start arguments born of your insecurity.

What's happened? You have joined your friend in faultfinding and now you see only the flaws. Instead of supporting your mate's good qualities with positive reinforcement, you nag your mate about the things you don't like.

All too soon you are dissatisfied with this new relationship and you painfully call it off. Trying to look on the bright side, you congratulate yourself for listening to your friend, who warned you that it wouldn't last.

This type of sabotage goes on all the time, and can be related to your job, your kids, your parents or any other aspect of your life where you are emotionally involved and hoping for a positive outcome.

But it doesn't have to be this way. You don't have to fall victim to negative people who promote an agenda of failure. And you don't have to worry all the time.

Worry is the opposite of hope.

Both emotions – worry and hope – are projected by your mind from the present into the future. With a hopeful outlook you remain positive and happy, knowing that no matter what is next around the corner in your life, you'll be able to handle it. You maintain optimism that your life will be a good one.

When you worry, on the other hand, you envision the future in great detail, and it's all bad. Your fears take over and paint a dark picture of what is to come. You fret in your mind as if all your imaginings about "tomorrow" are actually real.

And yet they are not real. They are merely anxious thoughts in your head.

That's how powerful the human mind is. We are capable of dreaming up events that have not happened and getting so wrapped up in the emotions that our bodies believe it is all real.

Chronic stress kills. (Take a look at the list of stress-related diseases in Chapter Nine of my stress management book, "Forget Your Troubles: Enjoy Your Life Today.")

To be happy, you must give yourself relief from the stress burden you carry, or it will shorten your life. At the end of each day, at the very least, set down your burden, firmly tell yourself that you will deal with the rest of it tomorrow, and get a good night's rest.

Grab a cheerful outlook

Smile. The simple act of smiling makes a huge difference in anyone's life. The muscles that lift your mouth send an instant message to your brain that you are smiling. Thousands of impressions from all the memories filed away in your brain join together to define that smile as a sign you are happy.

So go ahead and trick yourself into acting happy about your life even if there's a lot of chaos going on, or tough times to endure.

Frowning only makes matters worse. Grousing constantly about how bad things are actually make them harder to cope with.

Lighten things up by taking a positive and cheerful attitude and making it your own. It doesn't mean that you dismiss your problems or put on an artificial "Who cares!" expression or flippant behavior.

What a cheerful outlook can do for you is help you remember that life is a magnificent journey. Like a rose garden, life has beauty, glory and peace... and sometimes it also has bugs, disease, thorns and rainfall.

Make a decision

Are you ready to take this a step further? Do you want to have happiness in your heart all the time, for the rest of your life?

It only requires this: decide that you will be happy.

Yes, it's that simple and that powerful. What you do with this momentous decision is to drastically shift the way you approach your life.

You now have a new course to follow. I believe we are all meant to be truly happy, even though the lessons we need to learn in our lifetimes can often be hard and painful.

Each day, in whatever happens, quietly remind yourself: "I choose happiness."

When you are having a bad day, and realize that your thoughts are gloomy, dark and pessimistic, breathe slowly to calm yourself. Get back on track with a firm reminder that you made a decision to have a lifetime of happiness. Hold onto that decision, and don't let go.

In upcoming chapters, I'll teach you exactly what to do with your decision and how to make it work for you, in accordance with the 7 Powers of Happiness that you're going to learn.

Don't worry at this point about the "how" part. Make the decision "I choose happiness" and repeat it to yourself daily, to establish it within your own heart and soul.

Get centered

When you find yourself upset or worried, get centered again in an optimistic outlook. As we discussed in the previous chapter, you can achieve lasting peace of mind when you choose to be grateful about your life.

By centering yourself so that you slough off the negative aspects around you, you can be strong no matter what's happening. This process is particularly important to learn if you have a lifelong habit of worrying constantly.

One of the main problems with worry is that instead of being centered in your strengths and your best nature, your energy is scattered and unfocused. You become weaker, because your thoughts flit here and there, worrying first about one thing and then another.

When you harness all your power and energy and focus it on remaining centered, you gradually develop a strong inner core.

You can feel its presence within you, as if the heart of you is a center of light and strength.

Practice the sensation of having a brilliant core in the center of your trunk. Once you locate the feeling, whenever you feel under attack, you can mentally focus on that core. Reclaim the sensation that you are grounded in your own positive power.

Immerse yourself in happiness

When you want to make life happier, a quick change to make is to be around happy, like-minded people. You will probably find that they are interested in spiritual and emotional growth, and that they enjoy lively conversations about how to handle in a healthy way all the various difficulties that life presents.

Rather than focusing only on the problem, they dive into possibilities for solutions.

If they realize they've gotten caught up in talking too much about a problem that they've already discussed in exhaustive detail, they might catch themselves or be open to someone else pointing out, "Hey, what about looking at how you can resolve this situation? What do you think you could start changing right now in the way you are approaching it?"

People who are happy, positive and interested in their growth are not magically better than others, but they have learned the techniques of happiness:

- Surround yourself with happy people who have a positive outlook.

- Talk over your difficulties, but only enough to grasp the essence of the problem without slipping into whining, complaining and blaming.

- Seek creative solutions.

- Remain pro-active in your life, rather than passively drifting.

Analyze the situation

Why are you unhappy and worried? Is it a general feeling of uneasiness about your future, or is there a specific thing going on in your life that has you anxious?

It's important to take the time to notice if you are always in a worried state of mind. That indicates that your outlook is pessimistic. Probably without realizing it, you gravitate towards seeing the worst outcome for everything that happens to you, or that you imagine might happen next.

To counteract general anxiety and chronic worrying, adopt an optimistic viewpoint. Remind yourself of all the times that you worried about a specific incident and yet it turned out far better than the dark results you had predicted.

You can waste your entire life worrying about things that never happen – and what a shame it is to fill your days with anxiety instead of happiness.

Worrying is so common that even small children do it, because they are taught it not only by example from others around them, but from direct messages.

For example, you might take your child to visit a neighbor. During the course of conversation, the neighbor finds out your child is taking a test the next day at school.

Measure the potential affect on your child by comparing these two scenes:

In the first one, your neighbor immediately makes a tutting sound and frowns. He turns to your child and says gravely, "I hope you don't fail that test. I bet you didn't study enough, did you? You'll have to cram harder before you go to bed. School is a necessary evil to prepare for life so you can get a decent job. Enjoy your childhood because things get worse from here on out."

Or, if your neighbor is more aware of the damage that anxiety and uncertainty can do to a young mind, he would say with an encouraging smile, "I bet you'll do great! School is fun, isn't it? I love learning new things, don't you? What's your favorite subject?"

I'm sure you can see that your child would be much better off in the second scene, but how often do we actually get that choice? Many times, someone rattles off negative comments and as you try to interject something in a more positive vein, they purse their lips and accuse you of being out of touch with reality.

Frankly, the choice is up to you. But when you see the difference between going through life worry-free and happy, compared to feeling uncertain about yourself and playing it safe to avoid too much risk... well, which life is the richer and more satisfying?

I think you'll agree that learning to handle life from the standpoint of being a positive and cheerful person makes the road far smoother than nervously anticipating problems and disaster at every turn.

What you anticipate is what you will find, because you won't notice anything else.

That works in your favor if you're willing to shift your thinking to expect great things in life. You'll be able to view setbacks and temporary failures as being part of the process, instead of getting discouraged and quitting.

Greet the day!

How do you feel about mornings? Do you resent having to get up? Do you hate your job? Do you grumble to yourself that it's probably going to be another rotten day at work?

The whole time you're getting dressed, are you already living in dread and imagining the hours stretching ahead of you? Do you fill in the details of events and conversations that you haven't even lived yet, and all of them are boring, anxiety-ridden or disappointing?

If those are your true feelings, why do you keep going to that job? Even if it's not practical to get a different one at this time, you can find a way to enjoy the one you have and seek satisfaction in it.

You may find that changing your attitude is the only trick that's needed to shift your perspective so that the job becomes more pleasant.

Test yourself for a week by telling yourself repeatedly, "I enjoy my job." That's all. Just a simple, positive statement. Each time you catch yourself grumbling, stop your thoughts immediately and replace them with your new affirmation: "I enjoy my job."

Tell this to others around you as well. Say it out loud to a coworker. They may shoot back a rejoinder such as, "Since when!" But all you need to do is smile and say with an amused shrug, "I enjoy my job."

No need to defend your statement. It's your new attitude! And it will make going to work far more pleasant for you and everyone in your life.

There's more about the power of living <u>in joy</u> coming up in "Chapter 19, Enjoy."

You can use this same idea of "I enjoy..." to shift your attitude about any part of your life routine that you are not crazy about but that you cannot change due to practical constraints (such as needing the paycheck or needing to take care of someone else as a responsible adult).

Anything in your life that you dislike or even hate can be magically turned around to be more bearable or enjoyable when you focus on giving yourself positive, life-affirming messages about it.

Replace those critical thoughts with happy ones, and do it now before the anxiety and worry habit makes you sick.

Jump start your morning

As part of your new attitude toward life, practice a 3-step approach to each new day of your life:

1. Be calm,
2. Be centered and
3. Be relaxed.

Spice up your life by going out more often or trying a new hobby. Give yourself a pep talk and remind yourself that you're never too old to do new and exciting things.

We all love to be surrounded by cheerful people, because they make us feel happier about ourselves too. Some people spread sunshine wherever they are, and you can learn to copy their attitude.

One of the reasons why these people are cheerful is because they feel satisfied with their lives – not because they have everything they desire in material goods or success but because they are contented with what they do have. They don't fret over the things they are lacking.

Learn to be happy with what you have, and you will learn a major secret to being cheerful and upbeat.

Enjoy the people around you without trying to control or improve them. This makes for a happy and comfortable disposition. Avoid feeling scared or fearful about things that you have no control over. Learn to play and have fun with life, enjoying all the small pleasures in each day.

Fear is a negative feeling that gets you nowhere.

Chapter 6 – Action Steps: Don't be fearful, be cheerful

1. Relax. Life is not a timed scholastic test that you must frantically finish. Take a moment to reflect on your many blessings and be happy that you have this new day in front of you that you have not yet filled.

2. An old saying goes, "This is the first day of the rest of your life." So make it a good one! Don't waste it on worries about the future. The "future" is an imaginary time that never exists. All we have is this "moment" – the present. It is truly a gift. Enjoy it to the fullest, so that you know you spent the time well and did not waste it.

3. Greet each day with a smile, starting with a smile to yourself in the bathroom mirror. "Hello, human! Enjoy the new day!"

4. Keep your mind open to new adventures and new experiences. These don't have to be on a grand scale. The small, simple pleasures of life are memorable and satisfying. Try something new for breakfast or lunch. Take a different route to work or to the stores where you need to do errands. Call out a "Hi, how are you today?" to people you meet or

cross paths with. Don't shortchange yourself by refusing to acknowledge those you think are beneath you in some way. Setting yourself up as socially superior only limits the wonderful conversations that you can have, sometimes in the most unlikely places with surprising people.

5. Remember your new motto: Don't worry, be happy! There's a song by that title, made famous by Bobby McFerrin. Meher Baba, an Indian mystic who died in 1969 said, "Do your best. Then, don't worry. Be happy in my love. I will help you." After that, "Don't worry, be happy" became a popular saying, and McFerrin used it for his song. If you know the tune, whistle or sing it and make it your new theme song. Your cheerful attitude will be contagious. Others around you will be happier too. It's a powerful feeling to know you can spread joy. Now go out there and do it.

Part Two

Life Is a Beach

Chapter 7

Weather the Storms

If you've led a charmed life up until now, don't be taken by surprise when things abruptly change, because there will be storms. It's inevitable. But you can prepare for them, and in this chapter, I'll explain exactly how to do that.

Don't take it personally

In the midst of a tornado or fire, most people are so grateful for their saved lives that their destroyed house and material goods lose priority. Of course they wish they still had their things, but they weathered the storm and came out the other side with a strong value about what is most important to them: their family and friends.

For most of us, the storms in our lives are not physical acts of nature but rather various difficulties and challenges that seem to attack us from nowhere. These might be:

- Losing your job.
- A sudden illness in the family.
- A serious car accident.
- An injury that leaves you disabled in some way, temporarily or permanently.
- Your kids get in trouble with the law or at school.

- A relative or close friend dies.

- Financial setbacks.

- Something important you wanted fails to manifest.

- Divorce.

- Your best friend moves away.

The stress of life events can be hard to handle, but to lead a happy life, you need to learn that these changes are all part of common experiences, happening right now to countless others around the world. Don't feel that you've been handpicked to have disaster in your life.

The challenge is to accept the reality of what's going on, and then do your best to cope.

More coping tools are coming up in Part Three of this book. If you skip ahead, be sure to come back to this section – "Life Is a Beach" – because these six chapters contain important techniques for your happiness.

Handle life's crises

If you feel that you don't deserve to have bad things happen to you, then take a moment to define the word "deserve." If you base your happiness on an unwritten rule book that says "I deserve this" or "he deserves that," you are opening yourself up to disappointment.

If you say to yourself, "He doesn't deserve that promotion!" or "She's been so mean, I won't treat her nicely because she doesn't deserve it!" then you are judging other people from the outside. Stop doing it, for your own sake if not for theirs.

Your feelings of revenge and spite are putting you in the hot seat. Do you want to always get what you "deserve" for such mean thoughts?

I hope that's food for thought, because we often forget that when we point a finger at others, three fingers are pointing back to us. Use that as a signal to remind you to look within and see where your own judgmental or critical thoughts are at fault.

Look for the lessons to be learned

Inside every problem is the seed to its solution. An interesting concept, isn't it? And it's true.

Sometimes you can be so close to the problem that you can't see anything but its details, from every angle. Solutions escape you. You might toss out a few ideas, but they come from a place of desperation in your mind instead of being from your best inner self.

Take time to talk your problem over with a trusted friend who is not emotionally involved in the situation. They should be able to help you be more objective about it and more practical in your approach.

Spend time each day on being quiet and breathing calmly for several minutes or more. Release your tension with exercise even if it's running in place for ten minutes to give your body a change of pace.

Remind yourself that you will get through this ordeal, because you are stronger than the problem.

If you have faith in a God of your understanding, rely on prayer to build up your courage and ease your despair. You might even tell yourself, "My God is bigger than this problem, so I'm going to be okay."

Focus on what you can do "today"

It's easy to get caught up in the many aspects of a complex problem and not know where to begin. You might feel overwhelmed because there are so many tasks in front of you and all of them appear to be urgent. It can be tempting to throw your hands in the air and give up.

But if you break down the work required into do-able chunks, and give yourself a timetable – even as simple as jotting reminders on the kitchen calendar of important things to do each day – then you can tackle the project which the storm has dumped on you.

Each morning when you get up, look at the calendar or your note pad and see what's the most important thing to do this day. It might be to make a phone call or arrange for someone to come over and help with specific details.

Whatever it is on your list, be sure to do it. When you procrastinate, the chores will pile up fast and you'll feel snowed under again.

Do what's most important and let the rest go

In any case, avoid making an overly long list of every little thing that could be done if this were a perfect world and you had unlimited time and resources.

Instead, make it your priority to pay attention only to the next most important thing on the list. Let those smaller, less urgent items fall to the wayside.

Someday you might get around to them, but if you put time and energy into them now, you'll be missing the big picture.

Attend to the large matters so that you will feel the satisfaction of making progress.

Apply triage techniques to your life

Have you ever visited an emergency room? Or watched TV shows where a scene takes place in the ER?

If so, you're probably familiar with the concept of "triage" – it's a process of evaluating the incoming patients and then treating them on the basis of priority.

Thus, if you come into the ER with a cut on your arm that is painful but not life-threatening, you may end up spending the entire day waiting to be treated, while people who come in after your arrival are seen first because they are in more critical condition.

When your own life feels like a train wreck, use the same "triage" technique to impose order. Be ruthless about ignoring all the small things that cry to you for attention (you know that by "small" I don't mean your children or pets, right?) and instead put your energy into tackling the biggest crises first.

A simple example would be: a grease fire erupts on the stove while you're cooking dinner and flames threaten the nearby window curtains... but just then, your phone rings. You've been waiting all day for an important call. What will you do first: put out the fire or answer the phone?

Your automatic sense of urgency will prompt you to let the phone ring while you hastily throw baking soda on the fire or put a pot lid over the pan to smother the flames.

Unfortunately, our lives are usually not that clear cut and simple. However, you can get in the habit of asking yourself, "What's more important?" Then take care of that project or task right away.

When you systematically approach your life with the triage method, you will be able to plow through difficult things faster than you thought possible. You spend less time hesitating, and more time acting.

Procrastination is the enemy of productivity. It actually takes more time to put off doing things that are important than if you get started and keep going until it's done. Test this theory if you don't believe me.

You will not only be able to lead a less stressful life when you take care of important things first, but you'll feel happier about yourself.

Learn to roll with life's ups and downs

In the same way a sailor on a ship must learn to cope with stormy seas, learn how to roll with the waves and unexpected storms. If you don't, just like a novice sailor will get seasick, you will feel constantly under attack and sick at the way your life is going.

Stay centered in your core of serenity

Above all, during life's storms, keep track of that core of serenity you have deep inside. It resides in the center of you.

Visualize it as a bright white light.

When you need extra courage and fortitude, close your eyes and travel inwardly to connect with your core. It will help you feel serene and energized, so you will be able to handle whatever comes next.

Chapter 7 – Action Steps: Find your safe harbor

1. Whether the storms have hit already and you're a seasoned veteran, or you are just starting out on the ocean of life and

things have been smooth so far, it's important for your happiness and peace of mind to know where your safe harbor is.

2. A safe harbor can be an imaginary place in your mind, where you visit when you are under siege at work or in a relationship. Or it can be an actual location.

3. You might create a special quiet place in your home with a few favorite books, flowers, candles and soft music. If you play a musical instrument, your safe harbor could be to sit and play a favorite melody for half an hour, to help you relax.

4. Other safe harbors may be a:

   - Church or chapel.
   - Special place in nature that you enjoy walking, hiking or horseback riding.
   - Favorite restaurant or café to meet a friend, or to people-watch or to sit alone with a comforting book.
   - Library or bookstore where you can browse.
   - Promenade of antique stores and quaint shops to explore.
   - Botanic garden or nursery.

5. Prepare or decide on your safe harbor ahead of time so that when you are besieged by one of life's storms, you know exactly what to do and where to go to feel safe, protected and at peace.

Chapter 8

Sunburns

As you go through life, it's important to protect yourself from sun damage. You probably use a sunscreen with a SPF rating to tell you the strength of the "sun protection factor."

I believe it's even more crucial to be aware of your other SPF – what I call your "Soul Protection Factor." Let me introduce you to the concept.

Remember your SPF – Soul Protection Factor

Your newest SPF (Soul Protection Factor) is all about guarding yourself from harmful influences that will drag you down into negative thinking and nonproductive reacting.

Although there is no such thing as a "perfect" relationship, there certainly are ones that do a lot of damage. The following relationships burn your heart and soul, and are to be avoided as much as possible, at work and home:

- Codependent relationships of any kind.
- Hooking up with a bully or tyrant.
- Falling for a narcissist.
- Friendships with control freaks.

When you are aware of the need to protect your soul from damage, you will learn to be more aware of the warning signs when someone is bad for you.

It's funny how we can always recognize the signs in hindsight. At the end of a troubled relationship, it's common to stop and reflect on the details, trying to figure out what went wrong. You probably even admit to yourself that you did have several clues about their bad behavior from the start – but you didn't want to believe it!

Now that you are wiser, incorporate the concept of SPF (Soul Protection Factor) in your thoughts when you meet someone new or go on an interview.

Let SPF help your antenna be more attuned to whether the person is sending out danger signals.

Don't fool yourself into thinking that you'll be able to change the other person. Or that because you really need this job, you'll be able to tolerate working for this person even though they send up red flags of being a tyrant. Instead, what will happen is that months from now you'll be unhappy and wish you'd paid attention to your own intuitive warnings.

Holding onto pain

What is it about love relationships that keeps us coming back time and again, even after we've been burned?

It's the bliss, of course. The excitement of meeting a new person, and all the hope that goes with the early days of getting to know someone and wishing that this time will be better than before.

Some people seem to end up in the same exact pit, though, time after time, because they pick the same personality in a new body.

Maybe you've seen this happen to friends, or it might be part of your own story. And you wail to yourself: "Why do I always pick the same type? Why can't I pick somebody who'll actually be good for me?!"

Part of the answer lies in the fact that you have not truly healed from your past experiences. Even though the memories are painful, part of you holds onto that pain because it feels too important to let go of. Also, it makes for a lot of drama when you complain to friends and they feel bad for you.

You can also gain sympathy from the new love when you confide about how awful the last one was, not even recognizing yet how many similarities exist between old and new.

The hard part comes when you hook up with someone who is stuck in bad behavior and refuses to acknowledge or take care of their own problems. That's a dead-end, and you'll make yourself sick trying to change them.

The reason for painful relationships repeating themselves in new people is that you have lessons to learn. Since you haven't learned them yet, more tests of the exact same variety keep popping up in front of you. And this will continue to happen for the rest of your life until you grasp the question being asked of your soul, and learn what you need to know to move on.

For instance, the question might revolve around respect. Your lack of self-respect lands you in abusive relationships again and again. When you learn to finally respect yourself, you will no longer tolerate that kind of treatment. You'll free yourself from the cycle of sick relationships... lesson learned.

Or perhaps you have too many caretaker and enabler tendencies, and you land in relationships with immature people who lean on you too much and expect you to provide all their emotional, and sometimes material, needs. Learning to strengthen your boundaries and say "no" will help you get back in balance. Again, lesson learned, and you are now free to pursue relationships that will be more reciprocal.

Learning your lesson doesn't mean you instantly go from an imbalanced relationship to one that is ideal. You're not ready for it, and it would feel foreign. But as you grow, you'll naturally be interested in people who are also on a growth path, and as you learn lessons, you are ready for the next level up. You will seek out people who are at least on that level, too, so you can challenge what you've learned thus far by putting experience and theory into action, and keep growing even more.

Picking at scabs

Along with holding onto the pain of a bad relationship comes the process of picking at the old wounds so that, although that's not your intention, they can never heal.

Perhaps you go over each fight in your head. You recall every detail of the nasty comments and how much it hurt your feelings. You re-live each moment you can remember, and you do this over and over again, keeping it fresh and alive, as if the argument or painful experience just happened.

The human mind is unique in being able to do this. You can lose an entire "present day" by remaining in the past in your head while you walk through your life zombie-like.

You might show up at work and do your job, you might go out to dinner with others and carry on a conversation, but you're not really there. Not fully, anyway. In your head you are living a separate life, one that is like a film reel on an endless loop, covering every scene of a relationship that has ended.

Are you happy doing this? Of course not, but the compulsion to keep doing it is fed by the real desire to put this old relationship to rest. The common misconception is that, somehow, by going over all the details, you will gain an insight into what went wrong. And then you will be able to shut the door on it at long last.

Unfortunately, picking at the wound keeps it sore and oozing. You won't find answers. All you'll find is more pain in your memories.

Dirty wounds

While you're picking at the scabs of failed, flawed and stressed-out relationships, if you add in a lot of negative self-talk, you can make the wounds even dirtier than before.

You might infect them with messages to yourself such as, "I'm such a loser, no wonder nobody wants to be with me," or "I always pick the wrong person because I'm an idiot," or "I'll never find a job where I don't hate my boss."

Do you see how much damage you inflict on yourself with this dirt?

Now the wounds are going to be even harder to heal, because this time it's personal. You aren't simply talking about a relationship that ended, you've now judged yourself as unworthy of anything better.

How will you be able to achieve something on a higher plane than the last relationship, if you convince yourself you don't deserve it?

When a wound on your arm gets dirty, and you don't clean it and help it heal with ointment, it festers. You might even get an infection and risk losing the limb.

The same thing happens to your soul, when you carelessly heap dirt on a raw wound.

Why would you do this to yourself? It's not done on purpose, but rather because you've seen other people do it, not only your friends but in movies, novels and on TV. Popular love songs teach us all the wrong ways to approach a new relationship or to get over a bad one.

Pain and self-sabotage? It's what your friends talk about all the time. It's "normal."

Actually, just because something is done all the time may make it common, but it doesn't mean it's a good thing. Are you ready to stop doing this, and begin healing?

You're going to love Part Three, where I will teach you the 7 Powers of Happiness.

Meanwhile, let's keep on with more types of "Sunburn" that keep you unhappy and stuck, and at the end of this chapter I'll show you tips to get quick relief from your pain, including a 10-day challenge that will make a huge difference in how you feel.

Resentments

This one thing is the cause of a tremendous amount of unhappiness, so I'm devoting a large section to discussing resentments.

At the heart of a resentment of any kind is an expectation you had that went unfulfilled. You resent the other person for not living up to your desire, even if your expectation was never stated to them.

Resentments can have several causes:

1. Someone was mean or unpleasant or unfair to you.

2. Someone withheld what you wanted.

3. Someone else got the "thing" that you desired for yourself.

4. You did "all that" for someone but they only did "this" for you in return.

It's all about you, isn't it? That's why we often feel shame along with a resentment. We feel uneasy inside, and we know that these emotions are not in our best interest.

But at the same time, you probably feel entitled to the resentment. After all, you didn't do anything wrong – it's the other person (or organization, etc.) that has harmed you. You feel outrage, and justified anger.

The problem with resentments is that they burn you up inside. They eat away at your peace of mind and self esteem. An old saying goes, "Having a resentment is like drinking poison and waiting for the other person to die."

That is the crux of the matter, isn't it? When you resent someone, you wish them harm. Often this is a secret wish, and it might not reach your conscious level of thinking. As a result, you may have a vague sense of guilt you can't quite get rid of.

Bottom line is that you wish something bad would happen to them, to somehow make up for the hurt you feel they did to you.

Let's look at the four causes of resentments in more depth, because they stand in the way of your happiness. After all, how can you be happy all the time (no matter what), if something disturbs you?

<u>Someone was mean or unpleasant or unfair to you</u> – you feel that you were going along through life, trying to be a nice person, and BAM! this other person came out of nowhere and slammed you with a cruel comment. They cut you off in traffic. They grabbed the last poppy seed bagel just as you reached for it in the coffee room at work, even though everyone knows that's your favorite.

You had an expectation that people in general will treat you with kindness, and it didn't happen! Ouch.

<u>Someone withheld what you wanted</u> – either they didn't do enough for you or they didn't do it at all. It might be that you were hoping for a promotion, and your boss calls you aside and gives you a promotion, but it's not the one you wanted, or the raise is much lower than you had anticipated. You resent that a better title and more money was not given to you. In your eyes, your boss or upper management withheld what you were entitled to. Again, you had an expectation that was dashed.

<u>Someone else got the special "thing" that you desired for yourself</u> – this type of resentment starts in early childhood and remains a familiar one throughout life. It might be that, as a child, you had your heart set on a particular toy for your birthday. You don't get it, but the next week you find out that one of your classmates got two of them for his birthday. You resent that boy, and the bitterness settles into your heart. He got what <u>you</u> deserved! Life is unfair.

Can you see the pattern? Yes, this was another expectation, that if you were good you would get the toy. You were good, but you didn't get it. Instead, someone else did. Even though it wasn't exactly "your" toy that he got – he didn't steal it from you – you feel that's what happened. As you get older, the "thing" might be the cute classmate that you wanted to go out with, but someone else is their date for the prom and you resent that person for "besting" you.

<u>You did "all that" for someone but they only did "this" for you in return</u> – again, you had an expectation that if you showered someone with affection or did a very special favor for someone, or did work above and beyond the call of duty, that in return you would get an equivalent measure of rewards or thanks or a bonus, or whatever your mind imagined would be fair recompense. But instead, you feel shortchanged.

Maybe you did a huge favor for a friend, thinking they would then do the same for you, but when you go to ask for a favor they turn you down with a lame excuse. You do a slow burn as the resentment builds. Gone are the warm feelings you had for this person. Now you feel you see them in their true colors: selfish and hardhearted!

And yet what actually happened? You had a hidden agenda. You didn't come out and directly say to the person: "I will do this for you, if you will do this other specific thing that I want. Do we have a deal?"

Nope. Instead of asking for what you wanted, you had a secret expectation that they would magically read your mind and give you a bounty in return.

In all these cases, you feel like you can never be truly happy because someone else got what you wanted or someone withheld what you felt entitled to.

Now that you can see your faulty reasoning, you are on the way to getting rid of resentments in your life – forever!

The trick is to NEVER have a secret expectation. Sound impossible? It's not. What you may need to learn, what we all have to learn, is that if there is something you want from another person, <u>speak up</u>.

If something happens one day, and you realize that you feel disappointed, search your mind to find the expectation you had. You will find one, if you seek hard enough.

Here is why: if you had not gotten your hopes up with an expectation of some sort, even a small one, you would not feel disappointment, and possibly resentment as well.

Tipoff that you had an expectation: You think to yourself in dismay, "Oh! I thought that _____ would _____." Fill in the blanks with what you thought would happen, or what you expected to receive from someone.

For example, you might open a birthday card from a favorite aunt who always sends a generous check. This year either the amount is much lower than usual or there is no check at all. You find yourself harboring uneasy feelings about your aunt.

Explore further and you realize that you "naturally" expected the same amount of money as a gift that she's sent before. You felt entitled to get it, and you didn't. It might be that she forgot, or that her financial situation has changed, but in any case, don't let your happiness level rest on what other people do.

See how much simpler it can be to be happy all the time?

Reasonable expectations

Please be sure to understand that eliminating expectations in your life absolutely does not mean that you lower your expectations that another person will treat you with respect. That's a codependent relationship and we're not going to take that path. It's unhealthy for both people in it.

You can't grow spiritually if you are being thwarted all the time by someone who is a control freak and has to have everything their way, or someone who enjoys belittling and diminishing you to build up their own low self-esteem and feel superior.

There are certain basic, reasonable expectations that are a valid part of a happy life. They include:

1. Being treated with kindness and respect by others.

2. Being listened to instead of ignored.

3. Being valued as a human being.

4. Being acknowledged for your contributions to the home and work place.

5. Being compensated according to an agreement you made with someone.

Unresolved grief

A big challenge for many people is coping with grief. Whether you have lost a friend, family member, loved one or pet, and whether the loss is recent or in the past, grief remains an open issue for so many of us.

You might notice I didn't say the challenge is "overcoming grief" because I don't believe you ever do completely. But as you heal, the loss becomes part of your heart, sometimes hidden deeply in a special corner where you can keep your loved one close in a warm and healthy way of loving them for the rest of your life.

When grief remains unresolved, it can present a problem for you in current relationships.

You might hold back from committing fully to someone because you want to protect yourself from the pain of losing them. It's not a conscious decision, of course, but one that drives you to make the choices that you do.

For instance, a man who has recently lost his wife might shy away from dating women who are eager and ready for a loving relationship. He worries that if they do get close, something might happen that would take the new love away, leaving him once again bereft and alone.

Even if he's unaware of these thoughts, he finds it easier to avoid relationships by dating women who are clearly the wrong type or by only going out with casual dates he's picked up at a bar and has no intention of seeing again.

In such a case, the man may feel he doesn't deserve happiness, and the choices he makes actually do prevent him from experiencing any joy. He's trapped in a common dilemma and unless he changes, he'll continue to feel restless and unhappy while blaming it on the women he's meeting.

Chapter 8 – Action Steps: Heal your wounds

The same way putting a sunburn cream on your painful shoulders can ease the pain after a day outside without protection, there are remedies for quick relief from your soul's sunburns.

1. Contact your enemies and offer an olive branch. Rectify what you can but realize you cannot fix anyone else and can only be responsible for your own actions.

2. Forgive those who have harmed you, and ask them to forgive you for the mistakes you've made.

3. Write your worries in the dust with a stick or a small stone. Let the wind sweep them away. Or erase them with a leafy branch. No dust handy? How about a washable marker?

Write in the sink or bathtub, then wash away your words and enjoy the fresh start of a blank slate.

4. Meditation: Breathe deeply and calmly, with your eyes closed. Spend a couple of minutes on this exercise. As you inhale slowly, silently say to yourself "My pain ..." and as you exhale slowly, silently say "is healing now, so I can move on." Again: "My pain... is healing now, so I can move on." Repeat the slow breathing and the silent meditation frequently throughout the day, until the truth of the words seeps into your very being. You are healing now!

5. Ten day challenge – eliminate as many expectations as you can from your life, and see how much smoother and calmer your days go.

Chapter 9
Sand Traps

In the game of golf, a sand trap is a bunker or depression near the putting green that is filled with sand.

When your ball lands in the sand trap, it's hard to hit it out of the soft sand in the course of play. If you're a novice, you might hit the ball again and again, and not be able to escape the trap.

Even pros might groan when their ball lands in this hazard, but they know what to do. They select the sand wedge from their golf bag, because it will give them the best advantage to hit the ball onto the green.

In your own life, it helps to learn pro skills like I'll share in this chapter, so that when you encounter hazards, you know how to get back in the game.

Watch out for emotional sand traps

In the game of life, we constantly hit hazards.

The disasters that strike our lives from the outside were discussed already in "Chapter 7, Weather the Storms."

I feel the "sand traps" are those areas of life where we futilely try the same methods to escape our woes. In essence, the problem is of our own making.

It may seem brutal to say that, but I believe it is vital to your happiness to be honest with yourself, so you can see where you can benefit by taking a new approach.

Here are some of the ways that you might create sand traps for yourself:

- Error in judgment, even though you later remember you "knew" better initially.

- Inadvertent blunder.

- Stubbornness.

- Miscalculation.

- Wishful thinking.

- Acting in haste without getting all the pertinent facts.

- Ignoring input from others.

The good news is that since you caused the problem, even if unintentionally and unconsciously, you can also correct it.

When you're caught in a sand trap, reach for the right tool to get yourself out of the hazard and back in the real game.

Learn from your mistakes

In "Chapter 1, Paradise vs. Turmoil," we looked at the importance of noticing the various patterns of your life, including what kinds of relationships you constantly attract and what types of mistakes you frequently make.

Those are all your sand traps. The places where you get stuck and you keep hitting that ball again and again, trying to force a happy conclusion to the mess you're in.

Recognize that these "traps" are actually tasks for you to take care of in this lifetime or else the same situations will continue to arise until you do learn your lesson.

At that point, you will be free, just as the pro golfer is now on the green and hitting the ball to score a hole-in-one.

Another way of seeing it would be to compare it to learning the subjects you need to master in order to graduate from a particular course of study in a hall of learning. This life you are leading is your "school" in many ways.

Putting the past behind you

One of the biggest mistakes we make in life is clinging to our old failures as if they are happening right now in the present.

We view our life with hindsight, still blaming ourselves for the choices we made that didn't turn out great. Or for the errors we made in important situations that prevented us from moving forward the way we hoped.

You are not truly living in the "now" if you are still sulking or mulling over your disappointment from something that happened even an hour ago, let alone years ago. It's <u>past</u>.

While of course we can learn from our past mistakes and thus improve our choices now, what often happens is that people get stuck living emotionally in the past. They think about what happened, what they said, what other people said, what they might have said to make things turn out differently.

It's as if we get the idea that by doing this we can change what did happen even though we know rationally that it's impossible to change one moment of the past.

The more you grasp the concept of living emotionally in the present, the happier you will find yourself.

Letting go of disappointments

Maybe you were in a prestigious contest or competition and you spent months preparing for it, only to end up in second or third place.

You can't seem to let go of losing that first place prize because it seemed to be almost in your grasp, only to be snatched from you in the final moments.

Perhaps you relive this event over and over, even recalling what you wore that day and wondering if you shouldn't have chosen a different outfit, searching desperately for the full meaning of why you didn't win.

And yet, losing a competition or not finishing a race or not getting the promotion you wanted so badly... that's all part of life. Many strive, and few actually get first place. That's the nature of any type of contest: most of the people in it will be "losers."

If you rest your happiness on being "number one" you can pretty much guarantee that you will not be happy a lot of the time. Even if you do get to that pinnacle, you will be looking over your shoulder, anxiously watching for a competitor to knock you off your perch.

Strive to do your best, but avoid getting caught in a cycle of pushing for a "win" at all costs.

However, there's another way to look at competitions, without going to the opposite extreme of saying to yourself, "I'll quit competing. It was a dumb idea anyway." You don't have to slide into a mediocre life just because you didn't win this time.

But what about taking a different approach? Instead of getting trapped in feeling bad about yourself after losing a contest or competition, or failing to make the grade in some way, make a decision such as this:

1. Enjoy the competition itself, on its own merit.

2. Exhilarate in stretching yourself to do your best.

3. Strive to win but do not take it as a personal failure if you don't.

The only person you truly compete against is yourself. Many Olympic athletes state that concept during interviews. Redefine "winning" as moving further ahead in your own skill level.

If your goal is to get a book of poetry published and you can't seem to get any attention from editors other than rejection letters, don't give up your dream. Keep polishing your work. Hone your craft and write every day. Improve your poetry so that each time you submit something for publication, you know it was the best poem you've written so far.

If you build your expectations extremely high, to an unreasonable level such as thinking your first poem should appear in a famous magazine even though you are unknown, when your hopes are dashed, the seeming failure can cause more problems than anything else in your life.

Why? Because you dug yourself a sand trap next to the fairway and now you're lying in the bottom of it. You can't see the grass anymore, even though it is within reach.

When you have specific goals and dreams, understand that few people succeed at the first try.

It's more important to know that the process involves a lot of practice, a lot of taking two steps forward and falling back, but then picking yourself up, assessing the situation to see what you might change to make a difference, and trying again.

Time is a gift

As you go through life, there will be many times when you notice a shortcut to getting what you want. Sometimes these are great ways to accelerate your learning. Study with a mentor (see "Chapter 12, Lifesavers") and follow their advice to leap ahead instead of reinventing the wheel.

But at other times, you might be tempted to cut corners by doing things that are unethical, illegal or maybe just "not so nice." For example, if you arrive at your destination on time for an important meeting, but only because you angrily cut people off in traffic to do so, what is the cost to your soul?

What price are you paying ultimately for being rude and thoughtless? If you do that in your car, you probably do it in other places in your life.

Stop and think about what kind of person you are becoming with this behavior. How would you describe the behavior, if someone was doing it to you?

Expand this concept in all areas of your life. Be uncompromising with yourself.

You'll never be truly happy if you go against the universal laws of love, kindness and charity.

Quiet reflection and prayer

Since learning about sand traps involves learning how to look at ways to avoid landing in them in the future, it's important to make time in your life for stillness.

If you remain frantically busy with nonstop thinking and worrying about the details of your life, it makes it harder to recognize areas you need to change.

To get the most advantage from your pro skills, avoid these mistakes:

1. Not taking time for daily prayer or quiet reflection.

2. Rushing through your prayers, barely heeding the words because your mind is spinning with other thoughts.

3. Thinking of your To Do list during your morning meditation time.

Chapter 9 – Action Steps: Overcome mistakes and fear

If you have a lot of confusion and turmoil in your life, take time to be still and stop the endless chatter of your thoughts. For this chapter, the action step involves meditation because it will quickly cut through the pain and fear you are feeling.

A simple meditation that many people find helpful is to use the Serenity Prayer, which dates back to a longer prayer from the 14th century.

The Serenity Prayer is short, easy to remember, and the mindful words give you positive direction for handling any situation.

You can either say the prayer by itself, or see the breakdown I've provided below which turns it into a powerful exercise for boosting your happiness.

The standard prayer: *God, grant me serenity to accept the things I cannot change, courage to change the things I can, and wisdom to know the difference.*

Now let's see what happens when you slow things down and use the words as a tool to regain mastery of your thoughts:

1. Pray slowly while breathing calmly and being quiet and still, like a meditation.

2. Instead of rattling off the words by rote, and wondering why they don't have much affect on your state of mind, quietly request serenity, courage and wisdom. And then both accept and own your three new gifts.

3. Empower yourself to not only deserve these gifts but to have them in your heart and allow them to vanquish the fear and despair that keep you unhappy.

4. Here's how it works. Say the words in italics and follow the directions beneath each phrase.

   Grant me serenity to accept the things I cannot change…
   (Take a deep breath, be still and listen to the voice of love in the universe as it surrounds and uplifts you)

   I receive serenity…
   (Visualize your hands out, taking this precious gift as you continue to breathe slowly and quietly)

   And now I have serenity. Thank you for the gift of calmness!
   (Hold your hands to your heart, absorbing serenity)

   Grant me courage to change the things I can...
   (Deep breath, humbly waiting for the courage to be bestowed upon you)

   I receive courage...
   (Visualize being dressed in a shining suit of spiritual armor)

   And now I have courage. Thank you for the gift of bravery!
   (Hold your hands to your heart, absorbing courage)

   Grant me wisdom to know the difference...
   (Breathe slowly, knowing that the wisdom of the ages will fill your soul)

I receive wisdom...
(Imagine sitting on a mountaintop, at peace.)

And now I <u>have</u> wisdom. Thank you for the gift of clarity and understanding!
(Hold your hands to your heart, absorbing wisdom)

5. You may wish to finish your prayer by adding these words:

Please also grant me gratitude and willingness, and help me walk through any situation to the other side, no matter how difficult it appears from my perspective. Help me to learn and to grow. I am grateful that my life is rich, fulfilling and happy.

Chapter 10

Drifting

If you feel like you drift on the sea of life, pushed along by the unpredictable waves produced by other people (all those bigger fish in the sea), it may seem that there's nothing much you can do about it but try to stay afloat and keep from drowning.

Are you drifting?

Circumstances might feel too strong to resist. Outside events take up all your time. You race from one thing to the next, always hurrying and stressed.

It feels pointless to prioritize your tasks because everything screams that it is "urgent" and you feel under pressure to perform on a nonstop basis.

You're worn out, and you resent it when anyone implies that you should be doing even more. You're already doing too much! And you're so unhappy living this way, but it doesn't feel like you've got much choice.

And yet, if you take a deeper look, you will see that many times you do want to take an important action and yet you procrastinate. You don't always pick wisely which project to work on next, and you often find yourself annoyed at the end of the day that you weren't as productive as you could've been.

The guilt adds to your stress. And the next day, the cycle begins all over again.

What's the cycle look like? Here it is, and see if it describes your life: Busy working hard at a zillion stupid things – put off more important stuff 'til tomorrow – pour on the guilt – feel stressed-out.

Can you relate to this? Then you're in luck, because in this chapter I will share with you how to straighten out the mess you've landed in, and then get back on the right track.

What is procrastination?

Procrastination is a delightful tool we all use, some of us to a greater extent than others, and sometimes more often than not, because procrastinating allows you to:

- Put off someone else's request.
- Stay busy with familiar routines.
- Hold off risk of failure.
- Postpone a dream that is dear to you, yet scary.
- Avoid projects and activities you dislike.
- Delay work that's important but looks hard.
- Pretend something isn't urgent even though it is.
- Stall an unpleasant appointment you dread.
- Linger on the fringes of success.

Procrastination is both enemy and friend

How can it be both? Because you cannot say "yes" to everything in life. Putting off some projects for another day or for a vague someday is an inevitable part of the process of managing your day-to-day life.

The reason procrastination becomes an enemy is that quite often the project that is put off is one that is important.

Drifting is not in your best interest. It sabotages you when you can least afford it.

When you understand how and why you slide into procrastination, it makes it easier to avoid the energy-sapping guilt for this behavior. Why waste time on self-recrimination? Instead, determine that you will put a stop to this habit.

To keep a perspective, see procrastination as a delaying tactic that has unfavorable consequences. These can be inside or outside of you, so read on to learn more.

External consequences

The most obvious results of your procrastination will be things such as:

- You miss an important deadline and someone gets angry at you.

- You don't get your specific work done on time and therefore other projects linked to it or dependent upon it are also delayed.

- You might be penalized or fined for being late.

- You are unable to attend a function you wanted to go to, because you didn't get a ticket before they sold out, or you didn't allow enough time to get there.

- Your friends and family are chronically annoyed because they must wait for you.

Internal consequences

You may have recognized some of the external results. Maybe these things happen all the time, and you've felt the victim of it, not sure what you could possibly do differently other than clone yourself.

The internal consequences of procrastination can be even more disastrous than the outer ones, because they linger long after the outer deadline has been missed.

What are some of these internal results? You might:

- Feel guilty about it.

- Feel inadequate.

- Worry that you'll never amount to anything, just like your parents or teachers predicted when they tried to motivate you by scolding.

- Feel less able to handle your life.

- Want to give up, because the results are so pitiful and meager.

- Feel angry that everyone criticizes you.

- Resent anyone who asks you to do something with a time line, fearing you won't measure up.

You may also get headaches and stomachaches. You probably have a general feeling of anxiety and uneasiness that lingers day after day.

Bottom line: you're NOT a happy camper!

Procrastination and perfectionism – a sneaky partnership

Along with procrastination, you might discover that you are trapped in the world of <u>perfectionism</u>. P&P: the two go together like a matched pair and are often found hanging out in the same person.

Perfectionism tells you:

- You're no good if the project isn't done perfectly. It not only has to be great, it must be better than anyone else could do it.

- People won't like you if you do average work or you are an average _____ (fill in the blank with whatever it is, such as being an average "good cook" instead of making every meal a gourmet delight).

- If everything is not totally perfect, then you are a failure.

The sad thing about perfectionism is that it usually arises with a desire to please a taskmaster or tyrant in your life when you were growing up. Generally, this was an authoritarian parent or a strict teacher who let you know in many ways that you could only please them if you were an overachiever.

Unfortunately, it never mattered how much you accomplished, because that type of person will raise the bar each time. They appear to be incapable of praising or rewarding good work or good effort, and you suffer as a consequence of their own inadequacies as a parent or teacher.

When a child links achievement with their intrinsic value as a person, they spend the rest of their life either scrambling to do things perfectly and always feeling under-par, or else they dropout and become an underachiever like Bart Simpson.

How to cope with perfectionism

Perfectionism is difficult to get under control, but you can do it. (I know you can, because I did and I'll tell you exactly what you need to do to master this.)

You will have to be vigilant about catching yourself when you are being a perfectionist, and stop it. Learn to allow yourself to do "average" or "moderately above average" work, rather than A+ for every single task in life. You may find it helpful to say to yourself, "I give myself permission to do C+ work on this project."

The reason perfectionism goes so well with procrastination is that when you worry that a project isn't quite "perfect" yet, you delay completing it or even perhaps starting it at all.

You might want to write a stage play, but you can't get past the outline to start the actual writing of the play itself – because you're stuck in making the outline perfect.

Friends ask, "How's that play coming along?" and you mumble that you're still working on it. You feel ashamed to admit that you haven't finished the outline, so you come up with excuses about its being a complex story and that's why, even though you've been talking about it for ten years, it's not done yet.

Writers, do yourself a huge favor and give yourself permission to write a crummy first draft. Push on ahead with it and keep writing at least ten minutes a day, every day, and don't look over the work you've completed until the whole thing is done. If you stop to read over the prior day's work, you'll be tempted to edit. Put aside your perfectionist's cap and put on your creative one.

When the first draft is finished, then you can start the editing work. But free yourself from the twin devils of procrastination and perfectionism so that you can get that first draft completed. It's an awesome achievement!

If your dream project is building a birdhouse to hang outside the kitchen window, use the same method: get started on it and keep pushing ahead, working on it little by little without judging yourself harshly.

When the project is finished, praise yourself for completing it. That's a great accomplishment, whether it's knitting your first sweater, learning a new backhand stroke for your tennis game, or baking a loaf of bread.

If you find yourself noticing only the flaws, be stern with yourself and dismiss that criticism. Understand the voice is not yours, but one you've imitated from the past critics in your life.

Certainly you can assess what you might do differently next time to improve your project, but put aside the tendency to fault-find for the sole purpose of diminishing your pleasure in your work.

Break free from the shackles of perfectionism

Once you get past the anxiety of whipping yourself to a froth over every detail, you will find an incredible freedom in being your own self, instead of always striving for the unattainable "perfection" pedestal.

The rewards are many. You will find life more enjoyable, plus you will be able to get more done in a more efficient way.

In addition, your family and the people who do any work for you will also be glad if you ease up on your perfectionism because you probably criticize them all the time for not measuring up to your lofty standards.

Priorities

You've heard it already: it's important to set priorities. But when you're stressed out and overwhelmed with a lot of work, you often end up rushing from one task to the next, trying to keep everything under control and in some semblance of order. No wonder you're not happy!

It'd be great if everything in life came with a priority label attached so that you could instantly tell what level to slot the project into on your "To Do" list.

The next best thing is to learn how to recognize when you are procrastinating – because that is generally a HUGE clue that the task or chore is an important one.

These tips will help you prioritize your life and get it in more efficient working order:

- Make a list of the things you are procrastinating about right now.

- Realize those are your top priorities.

- Block out time on your calendar for your top three projects and mark them as "V.I.P." – Very Important Projects.

- Put the remaining projects on a "Waiting List."

- Watch how much time you spend on less important projects and give yourself a deadline for doing them so they don't eat up all your valuable time and energy.

- Speed up your housework and deskwork tasks by grouping similar chores and do them at the same time each day or week, depending on how often they need to be addressed.

- Each time you complete a top priority project, be sure to drag a new project from the Waiting List onto your

V.I.P. list so that you are always moving forward with the most important goals in your life.

Use the "WIN" system

Tackle your To Do list according to priorities rather than a) the easiest things or, b) the ones screaming for attention that might not be of top importance.

The way to do this is to rely on a simple acronym: WIN. This stands for <u>What's Important Next?</u>

When you truly want to "win" in life, keep an eye on your list, and focus on the item that is most important to do next.

If you must pay your bills on the 10th and today is the 9th, using the WIN system, you will make sure that "pay bills" is at the top of your list the next morning.

By using WIN, you can get procrastination under control, because you will push yourself to stop thinking and worrying so much about all that needs to be done. Instead, you will use your time more efficiently and do the next thing that's important.

There's no need to wonder what's important if you first take the time to list your priorities and keep the list current.

However, there's always the problem of chores and tasks that want to sneak onto your "top priority" list and take over. Let's deal with those pests right now.

Time wasters

It's easy to get distracted by all the details of your day-to-day life and lose sight of your big goals. But if you really want to get ahead in your career, if you are determined to achieve your dreams, you have to take charge of how you spend your 24 hours a day.

These are common time wasters to watch out for:

- Deskwork like email, chatrooms, catching up on social networks, surfing interesting websites.

- Housework that is not urgent, e.g. cleaning out a closet when you should be paying a stack of bills on the counter.

- Daydreaming to excess.

- Television and video games.

- Chatting on the phone with friends.

- Sorting magazines and clipping coupons.

- Doing projects that are on the bottom of your list, thinking that will free time for more important work.

The inherent problem with most of these time wasters is that in moderate amounts they are perfectly fine. But they do get out of control quickly, like little gremlins, and they take over the clock so sneakily that you might not even notice.

Let's say you have a specific plan to write a chapter of your new novel every evening, and yet – somehow – every evening you end up watching a favorite old movie that happens to be on TV, or a friend calls and you decide to meet for coffee. Weeks pass and you haven't started writing.

You hate yourself, and you feel guilty, and yet you can't seem to stop procrastinating because other things always pop up to lure you away from the hard work.

The more excuses you agree to, the less you respect your own goals and dreams.

Chapter 10 – Action Steps: Be a swimmer, not a drifter

1. When you value your life, and want to lead one that is happy and full of satisfaction, you will come to see that you've got to take charge. There's no way around this. You'll never be happy if you live a passive life that is ruled by others. Even if you have a take-charge personality, it can be easy to go along with what others want, because you are so overworked and busy that you haven't taken time to notice your dreams are slipping away from you.

2. Grab hold of your life reins. Otherwise, all the extraneous projects and chores will pull you along and you will never reach your goals.

3. Take the time NOW to decide what is most important to you. For some it might be their career, for many others it is their family. You may have a dream of being a famous dancer, singer or athlete. Or you may want to find ways to make extra money for a vacation or for retirement.

4. Plot out the steps you need to take, and push aside procrastination and perfectionism as if they are mere annoyances.

5. Don't let the temptation to drift stop you from swimming through life with vigor and enthusiasm.

Chapter 11

Pebbles

We all belong to a circle of people with additional friends orbiting by a degree or more of separation. Find the ripples of your connections and you will learn one of the aspects of lasting happiness.

How many ripples can you find?

If you went to a pond with a jar of pebbles and tossed a pebble far out onto the water, you'd see the point of impact and then the familiar radiating ripples.

Imagine that you notice someone nearby and he also has a jar of pebbles. Each small rock is a different shape, size and color from the ones you have, though many might appear similar or even identical.

There's another person over there – and yet another, but you all have different pebbles.

Notice that the pebbles are in varying sizes and colors according to the person's talents, abilities and temperament. It's as if all humans are tossing pebbles into the waters of life.

The pebbles create ripples and eventually those ripples touch each other. Another ripple intersects the arc of yours, widens outwards and then touches someone else's ripples and impacts their life.

Each of us is connected through one or more specific types of interdependency. This connection includes friendship, kinship, romantic relationships or common interests.

A person is an individual unit within this network of people and he is tied through the kind of relationship he has with others. If we look closely into all these relationships, we can see that social networks operate in different levels.

Such connections also result in ripples that play an important role in how problems are solved, organization and businesses are managed as well as the degree to which a person succeeds in achieving their goals and dreams in life.

Researchers have found that happiness tends to be associated in social networks. The study showed that when you are happy, your close friends have a 25 percent higher chance of being happy themselves. Certain clusters of happy and unhappy people were discerned within the studied networks, and they were found to be within three degrees of separation.

Your social network (what's missing?)

If you can imagine a life where you sit at your computer and never go outside to see another human being then you should know what is missing. This is the world that social networking sites can lure you into. Social networking has been arguably the most popular trend on the internet over the past several years.

The irony is that social networking is anything but social in the traditional sense. But as time goes by, we have grown used to the idea that we can do activities such as play games, collaborate on work, and chat or share messages online. Many times it is even more convenient than doing it in person.

Visiting by text messages or in a chat room all day is not the same as being in a physical room with your friends. Social networking can never replace the special interaction of being able to talk one-on-one, relate to each other, give each other a hug, learn to read each other's moods and be there to offer support.

Seek what you have in common with others

To meet new people, you might go to a party, a business social event, a friend's potluck dinner, or other events. These activities widen your social circle and make your life more interesting.

New friends will open up to you if you tell them about your interests and share your stories with them. As long as you keep an open interchange, you are bound to find common ground with others. Keep in mind that there are many friendly people around.

Studies show that happy people with a positive mental attitude usually have the following points in common:

- Whether they belong to an organized religion, or simply believe in the power of prayer or positive energy, having a spiritual belief system results in a longer life and fewer bouts of depression.

- People who get plenty of affectionate give and take, give praise, help others, have friendly interactions with the store cashier and a loving exchange with a friend on the phone now and then, are also generally cheerful.

- They stay happily busy with projects that are satisfying.

- They make the best of life's trials and have a sense of purpose in life.

Reconnect with meaningful relationships

There are times when we wonder whatever happened to our best friend from junior high or perhaps your high school sweetheart. Life takes people in different directions, and it is easy to lose touch.

Reconnecting with meaningful relationships can be a rewarding experience. If you find yourself thinking about the people you miss the most in your life, don't stop there. There must be an emotional reason why you reminisce about somebody from your past.

Use the tools the internet has to offer to find your long-lost friend. A popular social networking site is a great starting point, as well as the classmate or reunion web sites.

Also, don't forget about the old-fashioned phone book, which may give you a hot trail to your friend or a family member. Picking up the phone and making the call may be scary, but go ahead and make the first move.

Once you have made contact, find out if he or she is interested in being friends again. Suggest meeting for coffee to catch up on old times. If distance separates you and makes meeting in person impractical, see if they would like to exchange email.

If there doesn't seem to be an interest from the other side, there is no need for you to feel bad. The important thing is you made the effort.

Many times in life, we move on and away from the activities and pursuits that connected us to friends in the past, and the old spark is no longer there.

If you are able to reconnect with your old friend, be a good friend to them. Give your friend enough space to get used to the idea of having you in their life again. Nurture the rekindled friendship by being interested in what is happening and what has happened in your friend's life in the intervening years.

Realize that both of you have grown and changed. Be willing to establish a relationship that might be somewhat different from what you had before.

Trying to painstakingly recreate an imitation of what you shared in the past will probably prove frustrating. If you still enjoy each other's company, though, you will find new ways to build the friendship and share special times again.

You might end up with a friendship that's even sweeter the second time around.

Discard or diminish bonds with negative people

If you have been around chronically negative people for any length of time, you know how they can affect your mood. More than likely you feel drained of energy or you carry around your own negative energy that you used to be able to shrug off more easily.

Whether your child or spouse has an occasional down day or you deal with a family member, friend or co-worker who is chronically negative, there are things you can do to remain positive and upbeat.

The worst thing you can do is argue with a negative person because this only adds fuel to the fire. A negative person will defend his mood or attitude and accuse you of trying to start something.

Remember that a negative person often needs love and attention. If there are other aspects about the relationship that are healthy, point out to your friend that they seem to be in a difficult place lately and ask what is going on.

You may have had enough experience with this person already to recognize that they always have a big drama in their life, and their general attitude is one of a complainer. Sometimes the best thing you can do is to detach emotionally from trying to change a negative person.

If necessary, you may have to end a friendship that is bringing you down. Life is too short to waste on people who create disharmony and fail to support you emotionally.

Value your true friends

There are key elements in recognizing true friendship. Avoid the hazard of people who claim friendship but whose motives are self-serving.

True friends can share their deepest worries and hopes and can usually talk about anything. They don't gossip or malign each other when there is a disagreement between them. And they remain in contact if distance separates them. True friends don't take friendship for granted.

This sense of loyalty is one of the traits that makes friendship valuable. Learn to be honest without being judgmental or accusatory.

When you have to walk on eggshells around someone out of fear they will get angry if you tell them your feelings, then it's not a healthy relationship. It's probably gotten one-sided somewhere along the way, and now you feel that everything has to be all about their needs to the exclusion of yours.

Seek a reciprocal friendship, where there is a mutual feeling of trust. It's important to your sense of happiness to be able to count on each other. Friends trust that even when disagreements, arguments or unpleasant situations arise, they can withstand the difficulties.

Recognize that there will be times when your friendship is put to the test. Being more understanding and taking time to see things from their viewpoint will keep you from hastily making a decision that you might later regret.

If you find yourself wishing you had more friends, before seeking new ones, look for ways to grow closer to friends you already have. Share yourself more. Open up and invite an interchange of thoughts and feelings. Go beyond the surface chitchat of idle conversation and really get to know each other, in a non-judgmental way.

When you explore going deeper with friends, realize it's not the same as abruptly blurting out your entire personal history while walking out of a conference room with a coworker. Choose your timing, and take it easy. There's no rush.

Plan to grow old with positive-thinking people

Fear of growing old ironically speeds the very decline you dread the most. And it will ultimately rob your life of any meaning.

Many people report that they fear old age will bring isolation, loneliness and lack of respect from others. Growing old is seen as a disease that can be cured or at least postponed by cosmetic surgery to mask visible signs of aging, and by medicines, potions and supplements to extend your life span.

In our youth-oriented culture, nursing and retirement homes proliferate and serve to segregate the elderly from the main population.

Should we try to reverse this negative attitude about aging and the lack of respect and veneration for seniors? What if we recognize and accept that the aging process and all that goes with it is a reality? Growing older is a natural part of the life cycle and it happens to us all, if we are fortunate enough to avoid dying young.

Common sense

You actually know more about happiness than you might think you do.

Most of us know as children what makes us happy, unless we've already been warped by those around us. We know that it's fun to run in the sunshine or splash in the rain puddles, and giggle at nothing.

So why is it that as we get older, we think "fun" has to be planned in advance, and involve money? Is it more fun to go to great expense to impress your guests, or to kick back with old friends and enjoy good conversation, laughter and companionship?

Sometimes all we have to do is stop ... put aside all the marketing messages and advertisements we've absorbed through the years that promote overindulgence and spending ... and use our common sense. Seek the connections in your life, and cherish them.

Chapter 11 – Action Steps: Create a ripple effect

1. Notice how your actions and reactions affect all the people around you. Use your power with caution, to help others be happy and grow. You'll reap the benefits.

2. Bridge social networking and actual social interaction by reaching out to friends for contact that is face-to-face and not just via online or text messaging.

3. Establish strong boundaries so that you can protect yourself from negative people and at the same time, send a message

to them that you care enough about yourself to seek a positive outlook.

4. Honor your friendships with unconditional love. Have a happy life knowing there are friends you value and who love you in return.

5. Plan to grow old with positive thinking people who will allow you to grow old gracefully and will give your life meaning and purpose. And plan to be the kind of person who will do the same for your friends.

Chapter 12

Lifesavers

If you feel like you are sinking in the sea, no matter how hard you swim, then it is time to send an SOS and reach out for help.

Be careful what you grab

When you're unhappy, it can be far too easy to get into bad habits by seeking a quick fix with comfort food, alcohol, drugs, excess partying, shopping and all those other things that can seem appealing at first. Maybe you've already tried that route and discovered for yourself that the glitter and glamour was false, and none of it made you happy.

Let's talk about solutions that actually work.

"What makes you happy?"

I conducted an informal survey, and similar answers popped up again and again:

- Being with family – doing ordinary things like baking cookies together, watching a funny movie or playing a game.
- Walking the dog.
- "Me" time.
- Watching my puppy play with a new toy.

- Knowing that I make a positive difference, and things are better for my having been here.

- Sharing love, humor and laughter.

- Art and music.

- Being able to create.

- Learning new things.

- Making a baby smile.

- Watching children play.

- Awesome quotes, lyrics, poems and prose.

- Writing in my journal.

- Just being.

- Chocolate.

Did you notice that most of the things people enjoy the most can be had for little or no money? The main components are the willingness to appreciate life and to find simple pleasures in everyday events.

Create a treasure box collection

Happy people don't get that way by accident or by sheer good fortune. They <u>make</u> their happiness each day. You can learn to do this, too.

What is your current way of reacting or coping when bad things crop up? Do you feel discouraged and defeated? Do you flounder in negative emotions because you don't have a <u>happiness system</u> in place?

Take time now to plan ahead by collecting different things you can readily do or turn to when life throws you a curve ball. Put these happy treasures in an imaginary box, or write down a description of several things and put the paper in a real box or in a notebook you can grab when unhappy times arise.

Be ready to respond instead of react, and you won't be caught off guard.

By thinking now of special ways to lift yourself up when you're feeling down, you don't have to wallow in bad feelings of anxiety and uncertainty when disappointments strike.

Here are a few "treasures" to get you started with your own special collection:

- Watch a favorite movie that is uplifting and inspiring.

- Take a brisk walk or play a vigorous sport to release your tension.

- Remind yourself of your lifetime goals, and take an action toward achieving one of them.

- Read inspirational books or say prayers that are meaningful to you.

- Contact a friend and ask how their day is going. Avoid discussing your own difficulties because that increases the power they have over your mind. When you do tell someone about a challenge you face, be sure to mention the solutions you are working on. This helps you stay focused on moving forward rather than stewing in the world of the problem.

Counseling/Therapy

If you decide to go for therapy sessions with a licensed counselor or psychiatrist, be sure to get references. If possible, get a recommendation from a friend who has had good results with this particular therapist.

Remember that as in so many things in our complex culture, counselors often have specialties. If you want help with your marriage, seek someone who specializes in that field rather than someone whose niche is teen counseling.

Before you start paid sessions, talk to the therapist on the phone and find out more about their approach and what you can expect in each session. Also discuss costs and the availability of insurance coverage if that applies to your situation.

Take a few moments to contemplate your answers to these three basic questions:

1. What do you want the therapy sessions to do for you?

2. Are you willing to make serious changes in your life if that is recommended?

3. How will you know when you have achieved your therapy goals?

I think the last question is particularly important, because you most likely want to avoid an open-ended relationship of going back week after week to a paid therapist. If you have a specific, measurable result to look for, then you will be able to determine when you are ready to cut loose and quit the sessions.

Naturally, you can keep seeing the therapist on a regular basis for the rest of your life, and some people I know freely admit they go for weekly sessions and have for many years. That's expensive, and you may want to seek other alternatives.

You might choose to see a counselor for a specific period of time such as four months, and then make a commitment to yourself that you will continue the behavioral changes they suggest on your own, with encouragement from a good friend or a support group.

Seek out a mentor

A mentor can assist you to do an effective job, advance in your career, or live a more fulfilling life. Their role includes coaching and training.

One of the most valuable things a good mentor can do for you will be to take an objective look at how you deal with your work or life. They often excel in helping people resolve difficult choices in their career or life path.

People also go to a coach for a crash course in time management, strategic planning, recognizing patterns and trends, anticipating concerns, honoring priorities and formulating alternatives to fall back on when things go awry.

Select an advisor who can help you balance the tactical and the strategic. This person could be someone in your circle of friends and family that you greatly admire, such as an aunt or uncle you often go to for advice. Ask if he or she would be willing to help you with private conversations over the next few weeks.

Other avenues are to seek a life coach online or in your local community. Be sure to check out their credentials and testimonials, and understand their pricing package before you agree to any sessions.

Pick someone who is wise

A mentor is usually older, if not in age then in experience. Many successful persons work with mentors. They may seem like they were born geniuses but the fact is it normally takes them many setbacks and failures before they attain their greatness.

Most of us are limited by what we think is possible. Find a role model who is experienced in the area where you need help. Your mentor already knows the pitfalls of what you are trying to accomplish and will help minimize your mistakes. When a mentor has your best interest at heart, this relationship should be a success.

It is unfair to expect a friend to take on the more serious role of guiding you through difficult times. You put a burden on the friendship because if they try to detach from your situation to give you advice, then you may resent that they are being bossy, or they may resent that you are leaning on them too much.

That is why an outside coach has become more popular these days, and you can choose to have only a few sessions or as many as you can afford. A good coach will point out the life skills that you need to learn and help you focus on what you want to achieve.

Having a trusted advisor with a positive outlook in life is a great advantage.

Friendship involves a different relationship that may not be part of mentorship. Although friends are a valued addition to life, your new mentor might not be a friend in the sense of being someone you'd go hang out with. That's not their role.

Don't take it personally if your coach is more aloof than a buddy would be. It will help them maintain objectivity about your challenges so they can offer useful advice.

Weigh their advice

Whether you get input from a therapist, life coach, close relative or friend, be willing to use your own judgment for the simple reason that no one knows you as well as you know yourself.

When you find yourself resisting a suggestion from your mentor, take the time to explore whether you have valid objections, or whether you are trapped in fear and reluctance.

Relying too much on the advice of others will defeat the goal of getting feedback, which is to make you stronger and more decisive.

At times you might get bad advice. Recognize that well-meaning friends can tell you about solutions they saw on a talk show, and yet it doesn't apply to you. Even a trained counselor is capable of giving suggestions that you sense are not applicable.

Remember that ultimately this is your life, and you want to be happy. Learn to notice when an option is not the correct one for you at this time. Thank the person for their time and concern, and file away the idea for later. You never know when it might be exactly what you need, further down the road.

But if you're paying for sessions and you find that more often than not the advice is not related to the difficulties you asked for help with, you need to take an honest look at whether this professional relationship is the right one. Perhaps you should end it before you spend more time and money for something that's not useful.

If you do reach that point, yet still want to pursue therapy or coaching, then seek someone else who is more compatible with your personality and goals. Don't give up just because the first person did not work out.

Stand on your own feet

Since failure is discouraging, you may think of it as negative but it's actually not. Failure can be an indication of the size of your challenge.

When you start to have a fear of failure, it is the death of progress. Realize that you can actually learn more from your setbacks if you're willing to explore the reasons why you failed. On the other hand, with success, you may get rewarded for the wrong reasons, which encourages bad habits.

It is a reality that your friends and mentors can only show you what is needed to reach your dream and support your efforts.

Understand that success comes with your own hard work and persistence.

Document where your time goes, spot time wasters and be ruthless in eliminating them. Incorporate these time management skills and use them to have a fulfilling career and a happy life.

Chapter 12 – Action Steps: Grab a lifeline

1. Avoid the lure of quick fixes like alcohol, drugs, gambling and partying when you feel bad.

2. Gather your resources so you have a plan in place next time you feel discouraged or upset. A collection in your private "treasure box" might include your favorite movies, books, prayers and a list of phone numbers for trusted friends.

3. A life coach, therapist or other mentor can help you go through a rough phase in your life. They can be your confidant or a shoulder to cry on during times of loss or failure. Know what you want them to do for you, so you remain in charge and don't fall victim to bad advice.

4. If desired, see a therapist for sessions to assist you in coming to a decision about a life-altering choice in your career or marital status.

5. The lifesavers you reach for could be a family member or a dear friend. They are the ones who will throw a life jacket when the sea you are swimming in becomes too rough to handle alone.

Part Three

Build Sand CASTLES

Chapter 13

The 7 Powers of Happiness

In trying to understand that "happiness is an inside job," many people protest that it's impossible to be happy when bad things happen.

This confusion is understandable if you stay on the surface of the word "happy" and define it as meaning you are glad about the present circumstances you're in. But let's go deeper.

It's all up to you

When you broaden your definition of happiness to mean a lasting sense of peace and inner contentment that rules your days, then you can see that the bumps in the road (such as falling off a ladder and getting injured) do not have the power to steal your basic core of happiness and serenity.

Instead, grasp this idea because it is true: YOU have the power. Only you can make yourself into a happy person who enjoys life despite its challenges.

That core of happiness and joy is yours to claim. Today. Right this minute. You don't have to wait another second to be happy.

Don't believe me?

Stake your claim.

Whisper it to yourself ... or shout it out: "I am a happy person!"

Do that ten, twenty, a hundred times a day until you believe it. "I am happy!"

Take the attitude that your happiness is unshakable. It might quaver a bit now and then in a crisis, but you will always recover because you have the techniques you need in your happiness toolbox.

I'm going to make it simple for you in this final section of the book by taking you through seven steps that will blast through your doubts and launch you like a rocket on a path of happiness.

The 7 Powers of Happiness

Did you notice the title of the previous section, Part Two? It's "Life Is a Beach." Others might say, "Life is a bitch!"

See how the shift toward a positive image of a sunny beach lifts you up rather than inspiring you to complain and, well, bitch about the circumstances and details of your life.

The power of an acronym

Sand Castles... have you ever been told to stop building castles in the air? That's what is said to people who daydream too much.

But it is important to have dreams. And it is also convenient to have a way to remember the new tools for your journey of happiness. Let me teach you an acronym.

The word "CASTLES" will help you remember these seven vital concepts of happiness: Choose, Accept, Strive, Trust, Learn, Enjoy and Serve.

Too many systems I have researched make it all so complicated. By the time you close the book or stop listening to the audio, you've already forgotten most of what was said because the nuggets of helpful information were buried under mounds of confusing philosophy. When examined further, the grand-sounding phrases shed little light on what you were actually supposed to <u>do</u> next!

I love sand castles. Don't you? They can be simple, or they can be elaborate. It's all up to the imagination and skill of the builder, the same way that your ideal image of happiness might be the quiet joy of being with family and friends, while someone else might envision a lifestyle of happiness on a grander scale.

It doesn't matter, because the techniques in this book are adaptable to everyone's personal vision or blueprint.

And as with a castle at the beach, you can always add more to what you planned initially, and keep on growing it day by day. Don't worry about your happiness sand castle getting eroded by the tide. It is safe from harm, in your heart.

The "CASTLES" acronym will help you remember the 7 distinct steps to follow for a lifetime of happiness and joy.

In the coming pages, you will learn these seven valuable lessons:

- How to make the right choices.

- How to accept the reality of your life.

- How to keep striving to achieve the goals you want and pick yourself up when you fail.

- How to place your trust in the right people and principles.

- How to love yourself and others in a healthy way.

- How to thoroughly enjoy your life.

- How to grab the golden ring by incorporating service to others in your daily schedule.

You'll build castles while you improve your life at the same time. Learn how to share your new knowledge with others to benefit all your relationships with my powerful "CASTLES" method.

Each of the concepts – the 7 Powers of Happiness – is discussed separately in the following seven chapters. A summary section at the end of each chapter will recap the top points to remember.

The concept chapters are organized in the order of the seven-letter CASTLES acronym, rather than according to their importance.

As you'll soon see, I consider "Accept" to be the first concept you should concentrate on when seeking a change in your happiness level, and I firmly believe that "Love" can be the solid foundation of your happiness.

Are you ready to discover how to put these 7 Powers of Happiness to maximum use in your life?

Choose
A
S
T
L
E
S

Chapter 14
C = Choose

At the heart of each new day is your choice of how you will spend the hours ahead.

Choose a path of happiness

It might not seem like you have much control over what you do all day. You have a job or school, you have a family, you have demands from other people. By the end of the day, it may feel as if you didn't have any time at all to call your own, so how could you "choose" differently than the way it went?

And yet, here's the truth about happiness: no matter how busy you are with work and other activities, it's up to <u>you</u> how you fill your mind.

Do you fill it with serene, calm thoughts? Or is your mind overloaded with stress, agitation, worry and turmoil? Do harried thoughts spin ceaselessly, as if there's a hamster wheel bolted inside your head and you can't dislodge it?

When you make the deliberate decision to <u>choose</u> peace of mind, you will achieve happiness no matter what's going on, because you will be centered in your spirit instead of being focused on outside things.

Choices in attitude

It's up to you whether you select a positive attitude to be your constant companion. If you do, you will find life's lessons easier to accommodate.

The litany of messages you give yourself throughout the day – what is known as "self-talk" – can help you determine whether you have a positive or a negative attitude toward your life.

If your mind chatter is all about feeling worthless, feeling that someone is out to get you, feeling that life is a battle, blaming yourself or others for your failures and predicting problems ahead, then you have taken on a negative outlook.

The irony is that you might describe yourself as being a cheerful and positive person, and yet your self-talk reveals otherwise.

The wonderful thing about attitude is that you can readily change it with persistence.

Create positive affirmations for yourself, and repeat them often, particularly when you notice that your self-confidence is flagging or when you feel discouraged. Here are some examples of things you can start saying to yourself:

- I feel better every day.
- I know how to relax.
- I am confident I will finish this project on time.
- I take responsibility for my own feelings.
- I do enough and I am enough, exactly the way I am.

Choices in action

Each moment of each day brings countless choices. It is impossible to take all the paths you encounter. If you go on a hike in the wilderness, you'll encounter many trails that branch off from one another. At each fork, you must make a choice: which way to go?

You will miss what you would have seen on the other trails, but each path has valuable lessons. Past events are lessons that brought you to today, based on the choices you made at each intersection you encountered.

If each of us had made different choices at every single fork in the road we encountered, we might not be having this conversation. But instead, our separate choices led us to meet in the pages of this book I have written for you.

You may puzzle over the endless variables in life. It's a universe of infinite choices and countless permutations.

But there is a quixotic nature to choice. Sometimes a seemingly trivial decision has monumental consequences.

Think of the person who decides at the last minute not to take a flight they were ticketed for, and shortly after the other passengers are airborne the plane crashes. There are few or no survivors. That person is alive because of their impulse to take a later flight.

Or someone takes a different path one day while jogging in the park on a whim, for a change of pace, and they get mugged.

Are these two incidents examples of random luck, good and bad? Perhaps. But consider the cosmic possibility that in each case you are offered new lessons to learn about gratitude and fortitude.

It's important to be aware that all consequences carry lessons within that will foster growth.

When you recognize it, you can utilize it.

You have the choice, always, whether you learn the lessons or ignore them. When you ignore them, however, the lessons will continue to pop up in other forms in your life until you confront the necessity to grasp something important for your soul's sake.

See how these choices might help you lead a happier life:

- Do things because they are intrinsically good or good for others, not just because they are good for you.

- Learn to consider things and respond rather than reacting in a rush or acting without thinking of the probable consequences.

- Stop judging others. Turn that attention like a spotlight on yourself and see where you can improve.

Guiding principle

The choices you make each day determine the full pattern of your life, but the hopes and wishes and good intentions aren't "you" – your actions create the real you.

So how do you go about making good choices? When the results are important, you will find it helpful to evaluate your decisions before proceeding.

For many centuries, philosophers have helped guide our thinking by explaining the virtues we should emulate. Acquaint yourself with the four ancient virtues:

- Justice
- Temperance

- Prudence

- Fortitude

They have not gone out of style, but might be more familiar stated in this way:

- Practice the Golden Rule: do unto others as you would have them do unto you (justice).

- Be moderate in all things, and forgive others for their excesses (temperance).

- Be wise and thoughtful (prudence).

- Have courage to keep going even when you are afraid (fortitude).

A discussion of virtues would be incomplete without at least a cursory glance at "vices" as well, since the greater the influence they have over your behavior, the less chance you have of true happiness.

These are the seven deadly sins: wrath, greed, sloth, pride, lust, envy and gluttony.

I have heard it said that the worst vice is "ad-vice" because it means you are trying to tell someone else what they should be doing and how they should be living their own life.

Seeing a list of vices or anti-social behavior such as killing, stealing or assaulting can tempt us to assert that we don't do any of those bad things. It feels great to be virtuous.

But what happens when we take a look at the more subtle ways we practice vice in our lives? Admitting to our flaws and shortcomings is a giant step towards self-improvement, so take a few moments to check off the behavior habits you practice on this list:

- Killing someone's spirit by hurting their feelings deliberately or doing other harm to their peace of mind and happiness.

- Stealing someone's glory by not giving them credit or thanks for work they did for you.

- Assaulting someone's boundaries by insisting they lead their life the way you think they should.

You get the point, right? It's vital to your own growth to be honest about your real behavior and not gloss over your failings and errors by feeling that in comparison to the truly awful sins, you haven't done much that is wrong.

Be ruthless with yourself. Look for ways that you are selfish, ungrateful or unkind. Notice when you withhold love or block goodness from flowing through you.

Self-examination is one of the greatest gifts we have, because it opens the door to change.

Simplify your life

Excess in materialism, busy-ness and noise are all harmful to the spirit. Find ways to get rid of the clutter around you. It distracts your mind and keeps you feeling unsettled, chaotic and unsure of yourself.

Each day, create quiet time for yourself even if it is only for ten or fifteen minutes, twice a day.

Don't use this time to go over your "To Do" list or make phone calls. Be still.

Spend your energy as if each moment is gold. You must choose to treat your body and mind well, or you'll burn out.

Trust yourself to know what is best for you.

Let's say you have a choice in front of you. It seems to be a simple decision, even though the matter is grave. Somewhere inside you feel a bit defensive about your instant choice. Maybe your stomach is aflutter or your hands tremble. Those could be signs that you are taking an easy way out instead of doing what is right but more difficult personally. Take the time to look more fully into the choice before you act.

The cluster of choices you make each day become your building blocks. Think of water molecules. One drop by itself has little impact, but if you add more together you can wear down even hard stones over time.

Molecules that are alike cluster together, and so do people. They become more powerful whether for good or evil.

Become a force for good. Join with other like-minded individuals to become a mighty deluge washing away the world's sins in a great flood of love.

Choose your friends well

Choose your companions wisely because they can offer support and encouragement when the road gets dark and you are uncertain how to stay on the path.

You can't be happy if you keep injuring yourself by being around people who are bigoted, sarcastic, discouraging and bullying. Even if you tell yourself that you are able to shrug it off and not pay attention, their negative energy will chip away at you inside.

Be mindful of the friends and coworkers you surround yourself with. Do you agree with their basic principles? If you don't share their set of values now, you will eventually, by being with them too much and absorbing their opinions and interests.

This same concept holds true if your friends' thoughts are wholesome, uplifting and moving towards right action. Stick with the people who are happy and well-grounded in life. They will teach you a lot.

If your basic personality style is that of a leader, your burden of choice is even more important because those who follow you will entrust you with decisions they do not feel capable of making yet. Lead wisely.

No matter who you are, leader or follower, look for the goodness in others and help each person you meet achieve their best self by relating to them in a genuine and authentic way.

Help everyone you encounter unwrap their layers of fear by showing compassion. You will find happiness in this process. Guaranteed. (More about helping others will be covered in the last chapter.)

The negative drain

If you are around negative people too much, it will sap your energy and dull your sensibilities. Even if you hold true to the core of goodness within, you risk taking on a dark aura of sadness and stress from the assault of negativity.

It is a rare person, such as Nelson Mandela, who can be imprisoned whether physically or emotionally by abusers and emerge triumphant. Mandela's life story is compelling and we learn from his example to seek inspiration in poetry and uplifting thoughts.

The dark negativity that we see so much of in life often appears strong and invincible because its adherents use bluster, big voices, loudness and bravado to spout their views.

Meanwhile, the virtuous tend to be more deliberate and steady in demeanor and less willing to do battle with the ammunition of anger, lies, hate, nastiness and sarcasm.

It may even seem that the dark side wins far too much because some of these negative people manage to achieve wealth and outward success. But in the long run, goodness always prevails over the short-lived vanities.

You might notice that it takes more energy to be around negative people than those vibrating at a positive level of love and caring.

This is why it is usually uplifting to be in a church or spiritual group. It takes less energy per person to feel good, not only about yourself but about others. The synergy of the group actually creates a vibratory atmosphere that is more powerful than the sum of each person's energy.

When you are away from that more spirtually inclined setting or group, it becomes a challenge to not be affected by the negative people you encounter. They sap your energy instead of enhancing it.

It's vital to replenish your spirit with positive thinking and affirmations, and with the joyful experience of being around others who also want to lead positive and good lives.

Limit your exposure to negative vibes. If you've already heard the news headlines, why listen repeatedly as the reporters rehash it, spinning each story to fill the time allotted on their show?

For each positive, there is a negative counterpart. However, the negative does not have to be activated in order for the positive to work.

Life is not a magnet or a battery with two poles. The two sides do not have to be in equal strength or otherwise the universe will disintegrate. Balance does not mean you try to counteract "evil" negative thought-for-thought like line items on a list.

By being good and positive you are not eradicating evil, you are preventing its proliferation in you. You spread good vibrations to influence others toward a life of goodness as well.

You cannot change someone else's thinking by doing good per se, but only by example through which they might then choose to create positive good in their own lives.

Chapter 14 – Summary: You always have a choice

Each moment of the day you make countless choices, some small, some more momentous. Together these choices shape the direction of your life.

When you are faced with indecision, pause and think of your options. Then apply to each option the weight of its importance to your Life Path. Will this choice move you closer to spiritual enlightenment? Or is it something that is expedient, that would solve an urgent problem but in a fast, sloppy way?

No matter if bad things happen, you retain your inherent choice of how you react to it. That's a lot of power to have, because it means you are the one who determines your attitude and outlook, and thus the actions that you will take next.

C
Accept
S
T
L
E
S

Chapter 15

A = Accept

Because of the CASTLES acronym, "accept" is the second power in your system for being happy all the time, but they are not listed in order of importance. I feel that acceptance is your number one key to opening up a life filled with peace of mind and happiness. It's the one to use first, to launch yourself on an incredible new journey.

Acceptance is the key

Why is that? Because without accepting reality, you live in your mind too much, rather than in the world you walk through each day.

To accept does not mean that you endure abuse or become resigned to an intolerable situation. Acceptance goes hand-in-hand with action.

Accept your role in life. When you need to do something of importance, don't hesitate. Step up to the plate even if your knees are knocking. Pick up the bat and keep your eye on the ball. Strike it with all your might, then run like crazy without a backward glance. Speed toward your dreams and keep going.

A life without acceptance cannot be a happy one. When you refuse to accept the reality of what is going on around you, you live in a constant state of denial and wishful thinking.

Be where your feet are

There's often confusion over what being in the "now" means.

Planning and practical concerns about future events are perfectly fine uses of your time. The problems arise when your thoughts are caught up too much in emotions such as regret about the past and anxiety about the future.

A simple technique for getting centered is to emotionally and mentally be where your feet are. In other words, where you are situated in real time.

If you are performing routine tasks, be on guard against the mental tendency to start fretting about what you will do next or worrying what next week, month or year holds in store for you. Generally, thoughts that are in the nature of worries and regrets prove to be unhelpful.

If you have a situation in your life now that reminds you of events you encountered in the past, then studying those past actions can help you to devise a better plan for today.

But if your only use for the past is to beat yourself up for mistakes, then actively drag your thoughts to what is in front of you at this moment in time, and give it your full attention.

Signs that you are mentally living in the future:

- You're nervous about an outcome.

- You keep rehearsing what you will say the next time you see a friend you've had a fight with, and imagining their response.

- You try to fall asleep but you can't stop thinking about all the things you didn't get done today or didn't do right, or that you want to take care of tomorrow.

When you make a full effort to keep your thoughts "in the now" you will find that you are able to go through life with more comfort and less stress.

Accept reality

Accept responsibilities that are yours, and be accountable for the consequences of your actions and thoughts.

Don't slough off accountability. No passing the buck. The buck stops here with you, in your soul, whether you realize and acknowledge it or not. Denial doesn't get you off the hook in the long run.

The reason that learning to "accept" is such a turning point for most people is that they suddenly wake up to life. They see how many times they've made important choices in a mental fog because they couldn't perceive the reality in front of them.

When you consistently accept your life for how it is at this moment, and you accept all the people around you as they are right now, then you can actually make informed decisions.

Otherwise, it's like tossing a handful of darts at a dart board, while you are blindfolded. Maybe some darts will come close to the target, but more likely you will miss in every endeavor.

By using this power correctly, you can learn how to accept all the bad stuff that happens in life.

Let's be clear on one thing: acceptance is not the same as saying, "I like this." You can dislike the fact that your car needs a major repair, but when you accept it as the reality it is, then you spare yourself <u>anguish, stress and anxiety</u>.

Eliminate those three things wherever you can in your life, and you will be amazed at how much happier you feel.

It's a great exchange. You can give up unhappiness and worry, and in return you get the abundance of joy that a peaceful life will shower upon you. It's all up to you.

Accept vs. Ignore it

When something or someone's behavior is unpleasant, to "accept" it doesn't mean you pretend it's not there. If you play games like that, you keep yourself in a make-believe world.

That's a common game for children. If they don't like a certain food on their dinner plate, they hide it under other food or a napkin and pretend it's not there. If asked, they will even claim that they ate it.

But when you're an adult, if you continue to go through life ignoring things because they are not to your liking, you miss out on the opportunity to confront situations and try to change them or change yourself.

You also cheat yourself out of the chance to speak your mind and present your opinion. And worst of all, ignoring the reality of someone else's behavior is a quick road toward being trapped in an unhappy or even abusive relationship.

Accept vs. Avoid it

Similar to the habit of ignoring anything unpleasant is to practice avoidance. In this case, I'm talking about avoiding something rather than dealing with it head on.

Let's say you have a problem with your boss, but you don't want to risk making a big deal and perhaps getting fired, so you shove your feelings inside. You tell yourself it doesn't matter anyway, and do your best to avoid being near your boss or alone in the same room.

Instead of working out what you want to say, taking a deep breath and confronting the situation, you run into your rabbit hole and hope everything will calm down all by itself.

Avoiding life leads to passive participation, where other people call the shots and you react to what they are doing but take few action steps yourself.

Accept vs. Judge it

A habit many have, which usually starts in childhood by imitating the adults and older kids, is to point fingers at others and blame them for whatever situation we don't like.

Blaming, shaming and judging are so closely integrated that we can talk about these "Terrible Triplets" in one section rather than separately.

When you blame someone instead of looking for your part in it, you get yourself off the hook of accountability. If you're skilled at it, you can glide through life without taking any responsibility at all for your own mistakes and errors of judgment.

Sounds like a sweet deal at first, but it means you do not grow emotionally and spiritually.

Shaming is another way to deflect attention from your own mistakes and make another person feel bad about themselves. In comparison, you look superior. What goes on under the surface, however, is that the other person, while pretending to kowtow to your control-freak behavior, resents you and will do what they can in passive ways to bring you down.

Certainly the relationship itself is dead, even if it keeps going to all other appearances on the outside. The person who is blasting out shame has effectively killed all affection between the two people involved.

And so we come to judging, which is at the heart of all the blaming and shaming. Judging is not the same as thoughtfully evaluating and coming to a decision about whether or not a particular relationship is healthy for you and is one you wish to pursue.

No, with this type of judging, one person has taken it upon themself to rip apart every inch of you and then fault-find. They take special delight in pouncing on a mistake you feel bad about, and ramming home what an awful person you are for having made that mistake.

These judges have incredible memories. They never let you forget a random comment you made five years ago to which they took offense. They dredge it up in every disagreement, until you are ready to scream. But if you dare complain or suggest that you both let the past rest, they will pull out a new judgment: that you can't handle reality and they were just trying to help you.

In actuality, people who indulge in blaming, judging and shaming use those tools to deflect attention from their own reality. If they can keep you spinning in circles trying to defend yourself, then you don't have the time or the emotional energy to point out all the things <u>they</u> are doing wrong.

When you feel that someone is judging you, learn how to speak up and call a halt to it. Don't let them get away with bringing up tired old issues that have been resolved long ago. Remind them that the reality in front of you needs to be addressed... and accepted on its own merit.

Resistance

Any time you resist something, you are not accepting it.

It's that simple a definition, but it is remarkable how persistent our minds can be when what we see is not what we <u>want</u> to see! We keep pushing and pushing, as if the force of our will is enough to literally change what is real.

<u>Reality is</u>. That's the bottom line.

If you want a certain friend or contact to call, you probably know from trying it that staring at the phone does not make it ring.

Yet how often do we do similar, self-defeating things in life? All the time! It's how bad relationships persist, because we don't give up and accept reality.

We look at the relationship and in spite of the serious flaws in it, we don't want to give up. We still want that other person to magically change into the wonderful being we are certain they are capable of becoming. We want so much to be happy that we pour tons of energy into trying to force our image of "happily ever after" onto the reality of a non-congruent relationship. It never works.

You probably have experienced how painful it is to keep resisting and banging your head against a brick wall, pretending it is a magic doorway that will open onto the world of your dreams.

Chapter 15 – Summary: Acceptance opens doors

Here is why you must latch onto the concept of acceptance and learn how to apply it every single day of your life from now on. <u>Acceptance makes life go more smoothly</u>.

That's it. That's the real reason people practice acceptance.

It's easier on your nerves than judging. It's less stressful than resistance. It's more fulfilling than avoidance. And it's a lot more satisfying than ignoring life and being stuck in wishful thinking.

Once you have mastered the happiness power concept of acceptance in your own life, you can expand it outwards. Teach acceptance to others in your circle so that there is more harmony. Do this by example, not by lecturing them or telling them outright, "You should do it my way."

If you brace yourself for confrontations and dealings with negative people, you will use too much energy.

Instead: <u>Surrender</u>. Go with the positive flow. Seek the main current and avoid the dark coves and the undertow.

A lasting sense of serenity and peace of mind can be yours instantaneously. All you need to do is <u>accept</u> the beauty of life and the reality of your place on Earth right here, right now.

C
A
Strive
T
L
E
S

Chapter 16

S = Strive

To fully grasp the concept of being happy no matter what is going on in your life, it's important to understand that it does take a commitment, an intention and discipline.

We've already discussed commitment and intention in "Chapter 5, Grateful Heart" and elsewhere, so now let's talk about discipline. Without it, the other two are useless.

The discipline of happiness

Many people mix up the idea of discipline with that of punishment because in parenting circles the two words are often used interchangeably, and yet that's misleading.

Discipline is comprised of training, rules and guidance. Punishment is the consequence meted out when you transgress those rules.

Reasonable punishment for a child who broke a rule by not coming home on time might be losing television privileges that weekend.

Self-punishment is rampant. If you cheat on your diet, the next day you are "punished" by the results on the bathroom scale and by being set back in your goal of losing weight for a special occasion. If the diet cheat was a platter of cheesy nachos with jalapeno peppers, you may add indigestion and heartburn to the self-punishment.

However, when you discipline yourself to strive for happiness, then you will choose activities that can result in being happy. It's that simple.

Set goals

If you don't know where you're headed, you'll get there.

Do you see what that means? You'll get "somewhere" eventually but the results might not be to your liking.

That is why you must take time to determine your goals by choosing the direction you want to go in life, as discussed earlier in "Chapter 14, Choose."

You probably know someone who is aimless. They may have a mediocre job that does not utilize their talents fully, and they are dissatisfied with life. Your well-meaning attempts to motivate them to pick a goal and get involved in a new job or activity leads only to a shrug and a "why bother" type of response.

But you don't have to be like that. You can learn from what they are doing wrong, and take a contrary action in your own life.

Give serious thought to the reasonable goals you want to achieve. Specify long-term goals, mid-term goals and the short-term goals where you can expect to see more immediate results.

Take note of the phrase "reasonable goals" because that is where many people sabotage themselves. They pick a goal that is far too broad and general, or one that is out of reach.

Again using the example of a weight loss diet, your short-term goal might be to lose two pounds this week.

The mid-term goal would be to increase your exercising in increments of ten minutes or ten repetitions every week so you are at a certain level by the end of one month.

The long-term goal would be to achieve a certain weight or clothing size in six months.

An out-of-reach goal would be to drop three sizes in time for the party you're going to next weekend. You set yourself up for failure and disappointment when you don't give yourself a time line in which others have achieved similar results with sane efforts.

Different projects require different time increments. If your kids are preschoolers, saving for their college education could involve fifteen-year planning that takes advantage of various long-term investment packages. But if they are already in high school you'd strive to put more in the fund over a shorter time span.

Gain knowledge

In reports from people who have had a near-death experience (NDE) a common event was a visit from a "being of light" who lovingly asked two questions about their life: "Did you love others? And, did you grow in knowledge?"

The chapter on love is coming up, but let's address knowledge now. Strive to learn more, so you'll be able to answer "yes" to the question.

There is so much to learn about so many widely different subjects, that no one person could gain knowledge of everything in a single lifetime. And no one could possibly be bored by the task.

Follow your own interests, and delve deeper. Start with a hobby or sport you enjoy and learn more about its origins and history.

Read more books, whether classic novels or contemporary nonfiction. Watch documentaries, historical reenactments and travel shows. Visit museums and attend plays. Learn about the world we live in, and the universe that is our home.

If you are curious about languages, research how language evolved, spread and changed into so many tongues around the world. Take advantage of the internet and learn a few phrases in different languages, or take courses to become proficient or even fluent in one or more languages.

Study various subjects in your spare time, for the sheer pleasure of expanding your mind.

There's no limit to the number of topics you can explore, so dive in and enjoy your endless journey into wisdom and knowledge.

Handle setbacks

How do you cope with setbacks? You can learn to pick yourself up and keep going even if you've had a long pattern of giving up too easily.

If you are not happy with your work or your career plans, take a look at related jobs in that same field, and see if there isn't some way to shift to a new tack while capitalizing on the training, experience and network contacts you already have.

When you strive to reach your goals, part of the pre-planning involves having a backup plan for when things don't go quite the way you'd hoped. Include practical planning for financial setbacks due to the fluctuations of industry and finance.

What inspires you?

An important ingredient in being able to strive for success and happiness is to stay motivated. Be sure to watch out for complacency and boredom. That duo will sap your energy and drag you down to the land of underachievers.

If you want to be a super-achiever, you must locate that special motivating force that will inspire you to keep going even when you feel like dropping out of the race.

For some, it might be that they want to succeed in business to provide financial security for their family and for their own retirement years. For others it might be that dream of seeing their name on a book cover or a film credit.

Remember that it is a personal thing, and don't expect others to understand or share it.

What inspires one person might bore another, so don't waste your energy asking others whether they think you've found the "correct" inspiration. If it doesn't ignite your own passion, then it won't matter how many other people say it's perfect.

You have to find your own personal driving force or you'll soon be faced with disinterest and you'll hate what you are doing.

Try, try again

"Don't be discouraged. It's often the last key you try that opens the lock." ~ Anonymous

And a side note to that an unknown wit would be, after you manage to finally open the lock I sure hope you don't keep trying other keys just because there are more on the key ring that you didn't try yet. I think they must have meant that it was the last key in the bunch that finally worked!

Consider the type of "striving" that is for tangible results.

If you want to run in a marathon, you would set your goals in reasonable increments. Join a group that is training for the event so you can learn how it is done. Make sure you have the right shoes for proper support, and that you stay hydrated. Learn what to do if you get a cramp or a shin splint (sudden pain in your shins) from overdoing it or from running incorrectly. Each day, push yourself to go a little further than yesterday.

By breaking it down into stages and keeping to a schedule, when you miss a day or you miss one of the stages, you can motivate yourself to keep going and not be discouraged by the setback.

However, if you use the temporary failure as a sign to give up on the whole thing, obviously you won't reach your goal.

If you feel discouraged, take hope from the lives of other people who kept going despite many failed attempts. The worlds of science, sports and invention are filled with stories of persistence that will inspire you.

Guard against complacency

When you strive to achieve a specific goal, you may find that along the way, you do get a certain level of success ... and you may feel tempted to quickly downshift your ultimate goal and then announce that you've met it already!

Of course everyone's personal goals are just that: personal. But don't shortchange yourself, because you cannot fool your own heart. Inside, you will know that you gave up striving and took the easy way out. You'll lose respect for yourself.

Your dismay at giving up your true dream will show up in myriad places in your life as you spread discontent to those around you.

So what do you do when you feel exhausted by your life circumstances and the situations you encounter? Focus on energizing yourself spiritually as well as physically in order to keep pushing ahead.

Two cautions

There are two things to remember in the midst of all this energetic striving: 1) don't beat a dead horse, and 2) be kind to yourself.

Don't feel you must continue pursuing a goal when it becomes obvious that despite all your best plans and efforts, you cannot succeed. There often comes a time with life goals when you have to re-evaluate your dream.

For instance, let's say you have been striving toward a career as a dancer and you have gradually gotten more and more jobs dancing. You've been making money at it, even achieving a modest level of success. But one day you injure your knee. And now, despite months of physical therapy, you have to admit the unpleasant fact that you cannot dance as well as you did before the injury.

The physical reality is that you no longer have what it takes to achieve the dream.

It's time to shift your goals. Not to give up on yourself, but to be realistic and funnel your energy and your dream into a different outlet.

Thus, instead of spending the rest of your life regretting the single dream that you could not fully achieve, you would brainstorm. Select other ways and means to pursue your dream of a career in the world of dance, perhaps by going into teaching, choreography or coaching.

This shifting of dreams frequently happens with age as well, especially in pursuits such as sports and dancing where a young body has a great advantage, and you must be realistic when you pass your prime.

Changing your goal mid-stream can also be reasonable when there is a decline in demand for the product or service you sell. Look at reality and realize when it is wise to give up on a particular goal. Even when others feel it as an obvious thing to recognize, it might be heartbreaking for you to accept. Denial prolongs the agony.

Understand that giving something your best effort and then admitting defeat when circumstances change drastically is a far cry from giving it a half-hearted effort and quitting at the first sign of drudgery, failure or rejection.

Be easy on yourself when you have to make such hard decisions, and don't pour on the guilt and shame. If you do, you waste energy and enthusiasm, and you will make it that much harder to pursue your next game plan.

Strive to have love in your life

If your goal is to have a loving relationship, then practice love in all forms throughout the day with a kind word and a smile, and with listening and caring.

Be a loving person in thought and actions. Make it a practice to spread love everywhere you go. Radiate love and let it beam out from you like rays of light.

Discipline your mind to be aware of others as fellow occupants of this planet. We are all on a journey together.

More about "love" is coming up in Chapter 18. In the next chapter, number 17, let's discuss the fourth happiness power, the one that is all about having trust in your heart.

Chapter 16 – Summary: Keep on striving

If you have chosen goals for yourself only because others pressured you to pick them, then you are probably not fully engaged or interested in achieving them. Your boredom threshold is no doubt rather low. It becomes hard to strive for what you want, because you don't actually want it!

The basic rule for remaining committed to a project or goal is to select something that truly excites and interests you. You are far more likely to succeed if you aim for achievable goals in an area that you are passionate about, and keep moving forward.

When you strive to achieve what you want, you also become disciplined about gaining knowledge and claiming happiness along the way.

C
A
S
Trust
L
E
S

Chapter 17

T = Trust

If you want to be truly happy, in my experience, you must learn how to have trust at many different levels in your life, and with many different people. Otherwise, you are going to be bitter, suspicious, resentful and unhappy.

Let's look at the happiness power called "trust" in further detail.

Trust other people

Do you maintain an overall trust that most people do not mean you harm? Or are you suspicious and worried that they are out to get something from you or put something over on you?

If you have been hurt and you've used past experiences to become wary, ask yourself if that reaction is still useful to you. Maybe you have outgrown it, but you are clinging to the habit.

For example, let's say that when you were a student at college, someone broke into your dorm room, ransacked it and stole cash, your new computer and a stack of CDs you liked. After that, you nervously double-locked your room each time you left, and upon returning you quickly looked for evidence of another break-in.

Normally, that kind of reaction wears off after the initial shock of the burglary goes away. But what if in that same time period your parents got divorced and your best friend started dating your girlfriend behind your back? Betrayed by four of the people who were closest to you!

The string of negative experiences reinforced the idea that you had better not trust <u>anyone</u> because you will definitely get hurt each time.

However, now that some time has passed, you realize you are lonely. You'd like to be able to trust again.

Where do you begin? <u>With yourself</u>.

Trust yourself

The foundation of having trust in others is to first trust YOU!

I believe that trust is one of the hardest concepts to master. Do not feel inferior or stupid if you have a difficult time with it.

Even great Masters in the history of religion and philosophy had to struggle with feelings of being forsaken, of being tested too much and of being abandoned.

If trust is a sticking point for you, recognize that it is an area you have neglected that now requires your attention. Remember what we said earlier: You must recognize it to utilize it. So if you want trust in your life, be aware that you need to increase it and use it.

This chapter will guide you toward trusting more. It is a process, and you won't get results overnight, but if you persist with the directions given here, you'll find that trust flows more naturally into your life.

Are you trustworthy?

Write in your journal or a computer document on the topic of trusting yourself. Here are some points to get you started:

- Do you keep the promises you make?

- Do you strive to meet deadlines?

- If you give your word to someone, can they trust that you will keep it?

- Are you honest in your dealings with other people, including businesses?

- Would a stranger at the beach be foolish or smart to give you their wallet and Rolex to guard while they go for a swim?

- If you were your own best friend, could you trust in you to keep a personal confidence, or would you worry about gossip?

See all the areas where you are trustworthy already, and ones where you could use growth.

If you have held yourself aloof from society for a while, or for most of your life, because you've been injured in the past, it might take extra time to learn how to be the sort of person whom others can trust.

Avoid the incongruity of expecting others to meet higher standards than the ones you set for yourself.

Demonstrate trust

Make a list of areas where trust is holding you back or causing problems for you. Don't waste time and energy on past issues that cannot be changed. Focus on today.

Start small. Don't expect to go from fear to immediate trust.

To begin, trust yourself and your own instincts. If you have held back from interacting with people on a personal level, or if you experience a lot of self-doubt, start by sharing your opinion about a new movie you saw recently or an interesting book you are reading.

One of the quickest ways to assert yourself in a beneficial way is by having an opinion and stating it, not in a way that drowns out anyone else, but by saying "I feel" or "I think." Own your thoughts, and drop your hesitation to share them.

You don't have to go along with the opinion others are stating just to be polite, even if that has been your pattern for a long time. Have the courage to say, in a friendly way, "I found that movie to be a bit slow. I'm glad you liked it, though. What was your favorite part?"

Stating your opinion assertively yet non-aggressively helps you gain more trust in yourself.

When someone asks whether you want chocolate cake or lemon pie, pick one. Don't be so passive and non-offensive that you insist the other person choose for you. State a preference. This small action helps reinforce your new habit of trusting your own opinion and your own mind.

As you learn how to do this, expand the process into more important areas. Dare to talk about politics with a friend. Let them know that they can trust you by allowing them to speak about their ideas without ridicule.

Notice that you will teach people to <u>distrust</u> you with these behaviors:

- Sarcastic comments.
- Ridicule.
- Mocking.
- Gossiping about them.
- Making fun of their preferences or opinions.
- Teasing about things that are important to them.
- Making them look foolish in front of others.
- Taking credit for their comments or ideas.
- Playing a game of superiority.
- Not showing up on time when you'd arranged to meet.
- Not fulfilling promises you made.

All those things will make the other person withdraw because they cannot trust you to treat them with respect.

On the other hand, when you demonstrate trust in an honest way, you will do these things:

- Listen when they speak and give them a chance to talk freely.
- Ask interested questions and pay attention to their answers.
- Reassure them when they are upset or worried.
- Show that you care about their welfare.
- Forgive them for mistakes they make.
- Remain loyal when others want to gossip about your friend.

Learn to trust others

Examine whether the people in your life have <u>earned</u> your trust. Are they trustworthy, in the same way that you want to be for them?

Have a plan for yourself, for when you meet new people. Listen carefully to notice whether they boast about themselves excessively. That's a sign that they might not care much about hearing your own stories or sharing the limelight with you.

Pay attention to how others react around this new friend. Do people you already respect like this new friend or can you sense disapproval from them? And if you are meeting your new friend's group of buddies, are they the kind of people you enjoy, or are you getting signals that this new crowd doesn't share your own core values?

When you realize you have a congenial relationship with someone, give the friendship or romance time to develop, so that both of you can get to know the everyday things that make the other person tick.

Don't feel you need to rush to the next stage. Allow the closeness to unfold as you spend more time together and share your thoughts and feelings.

A problem that many people with trust issues have is that they rush to find a new friend or romance and heedlessly hook up with exactly the type of person they found fault with before.

Trust problems are bound to pop up again if you don't take the time to pay heed to the warning signals.

For example, if you continually end up with friends and romantic partners who make promises they don't keep, who get caught out in lies all the time, who keep you waiting when you have a date for dinner or to the movies, then you need to stop and realize that this person is not being trustworthy.

If there are other things about the person that you do like, you may decide to give them another chance. Watch out for the tendency to keep giving "second" chances. You will be giving endless free rides if you don't speak up and let them know that this situational behavior bothers you and you would appreciate their addressing it.

Then, since their behavior is up to them and you cannot control it, if they continue to show disrespect by ignoring your requests to, for example, be on time for dates, at that point you have the choice: 1) end the relationship, or 2) continue to be their doormat.

Getting past betrayal

When the word "trust" is raised, many people immediately think about infidelity and whether a person can get past betrayal and learn to trust again from the ground up.

For someone who has been betrayed in a romantic relationship, you have a hard decision to make: whether the marriage or union is worth salvaging.

If the one who cheated is ready to file for divorce, then the infidelity was a clear sign the marriage is already over. It will be better for the partner to accept the reality of their mate's decision, even though it is upsetting.

One person can decide it's over and that's it. But both parties will have to agree to work on saving it, because one can't do that alone. Spending time trying to force or cajole someone into staying when they want to go is a lost cause, and one that will create a lot more pain for everyone involved.

If the one who committed adultery is remorseful and wants to make amends, then both of you need to discuss your feelings openly. It will be helpful to lay some ground rules:

- No name-calling.

- Focus on the behavior.

- The "victim" must also look at their own behavior and what they contributed to the deterioration of the relationship.

- The guilty party needs to ask for forgiveness.

- The other party needs to forgive the bad behavior with a loving heart.

- Both people need to discuss the process they will follow to get past the breach of trust, including an agreement to not use the past as ammunition in future arguments.

- Agree that you will not become hypervigilant and hypercritical of each other.

- Get outside help if you need further counseling to resolve the issue.

If you have a sincere desire to get past this turning point in your marriage and renew your loving commitment to each other, you must both be willing to see that holding onto the pain will prevent a full reconciliation.

Withholding forgiveness or shifting blame will keep you stuck in acrimony.

Agree to a fresh start, and make a concentrated effort to address the reasons for the infidelity. If the one who cheated did so because they felt neglected or emotionally abused, you must fix that part of the marriage or you are inviting a repeat.

Trust in GOODNESS

As you go through life, practicing the principles you've learned here about how to be happy no matter what, you will find the best trust of all is to trust in your concept of God, the Universal Source or a Higher Power.

If you have a hard time believing in God, don't let this hold you back from the loving support you can enjoy with a firm trust in the bigger picture. Why not add another "o" to the word "God" and make it "good"?

All of us can believe in the power of good or goodness, so put your trust in that. When you believe in the basic goodness of others, you can see their shining light despite poor outward behavior.

Do not lose faith. Trust in the universe to uphold you as it does a precious star.

Learn to use trust in God or goodness as your guiding beacon, to help you get through the days that are rough and keep moving forward on your journey of spiritual growth.

Chapter 17 – Summary: Learn to trust yourself and others

If you believe everyone has evil motives, that is all you will be able to see in them, as if they are a mirror to you. This view will confirm your concept of the negative rule that life is hard and just gets harder.

The cure: Open your heart to the possibility of goodness existing in everyone.

The crack in the door lets in a bright light to show the sun is up. The wider you open the door, the more you will feel the healing rays of love in your life, not by standing passively in the doorway but by joining in the love.

And you do this by <u>trusting</u> yourself and others.

C
A
S
T
Love
E
S

Chapter 18

L = Love

If you learn nothing else about how to be happy, please understand that the fundamental solution to everything that's gone wrong in your life is LOVE.

Love yourself, love the God of your understanding, and love others...

Love is the answer

Why is love so important? Because it is the linchpin on which everything else in life hangs. You cannot have happiness without love in your life. And I don't mean you can't be happy unless you have a storybook romance.

Enjoy "love" in all its broad aspects.

Love for humanity. Love for your companion animals, for your neighbor, for the guy who drives you crazy at work. Benevolent love and affection. Wish each person well, and pray that they get what they want most in life.

Don't forget to want all of that for yourself, too.

Often, unhappy people are caught up in looking at the details of their life circumstances and they feel shortchanged. They compare themselves against someone who has a lot more or who appears to have it all.

Use positive affirmations that are supportive of yourself and your goals. "I am happy. I am confident. I feel great." Saying these things might feel strange at first, but that only demonstrates how low your self-esteem has dropped.

Stop judging others

Do you have an inside critic? We probably all do, but some people have developed theirs so that it dominates their personality. As a result, they constantly complain and criticize.

Part of the pattern includes guessing what some other person is thinking about, such as seeing a pretty waitress and saying to your companion, "Look at her, she thinks she's hot!" You don't know what the waitress is thinking or feeling, yet you announce her thoughts as if you have the right to do so.

When you are around someone who does that type of critique all the time, it can be exhausting. The reason is that it is negative and saps your energy.

To combat the temptation to criticize someone else, find the essence of your best, most noble feelings such as love, kindness and thoughtfulness.

When it is difficult to practice these elements, remind yourself of the essence of love inside you. All it needs is one drop percolating to the surface to break the negative tension you are feeling.

The milk of human kindness nourishes us all

That "milk" is love. Just like vanilla extract, you can add a drop of kindness to any encounter, and make the day more delicious.

It can be confusing to see this if, for example, you know someone who has a lot of friends and yet when you two are together, you feel bad about yourself.

You question your thoughts and feelings. Since this friend is so popular, you don't believe that anything could be wrong with them.

But this "friend" subtly attacks you and lets you know in multiple ways that you are inferior and will never amount to much. A host of other negative comments stream forth, all of them designed to put you in the position of being the lowly supplicant begging for this other, superior being to befriend you.

You try to push aside your hurt feelings, and remind yourself that everyone else likes them so you must be the one who is wrong.

It's insane! Stop and think of what your "friendship" consists of, and realize that all the other people gathering around are not even true friends. They are the spectators this person has bullied into bowing and dancing attendance.

Probably this friend puts on a good show and is a good talker, always with big dreams and grand plans. They can be fun to be around. It may seem they orchestrate excitement, like constant parties, picnics and dancing.

They thrive in the spotlight. It can feel flattering when they pluck you from the shadows and invite you to join in. The problem is that their game is a deadly one, emotionally speaking. You're dealing with a narcissist who has no ability to empathize or relate to you on a personal level.

You will quickly discover, to your dismay, that all conversations must be about them and their needs, to the exclusion of yours.

So be sure to apply that milk of kindness to your own life, and get yourself away from people who are not contributing to your happiness.

Overcoming childhood abuse

If your parents or the people who cared for you when you were growing up did not do their job in a nurturing, healthful way, you probably didn't learn much about "love" from their example.

But it's never too late to overturn those bad memories and claim the love you need to thrive.

You can be happy now and have loving relationships of all kinds, no matter what your past experiences have been.

Take a look back at Chapter 17 because it's all about "trust" and you probably never learned how to have a healthy trust for anyone, least of all your parents, or the older siblings or cousins you expected to protect you.

After all, we know our parents are supposed to love and cherish us. So when there isn't that type of healthy emotional interaction, the child takes on all the blame and says to himself in so many words, "They don't love me because I am unlovable!"

It is that simple and that deadly to the spirit.

The child assumes the responsibility of the abusive relationship, and that is plain wrong. If you have survived childhood abuse, you had a no-win situation back then.

Unfortunately, with that background, many people find it hard to break free of the skewed pattern it embedded in their thinking.

They tend to forge relationships as adults with people who are abusive to them or whom they abuse. It feels familiar!

It can be hard – but not impossible – to break a codependency trap. Take healthy steps to end the past's hold over you. Fend off the attempts of others to make you change back to your old familiar self and get in your "proper place" where they can feed off your fears and feel adored.

There is no end to the abuse cycle unless you are willing to be the one who stops playing the old games in every single one of your relationships, whether at home or work.

You may even find that your friendships mirror the sick relationship you had with either or both of your parents. Your best friend might be someone who dominates and bullies you, and yet you continue to seek their approval the same way you tried to get parental approval.

Can you see the similarity? They are standing in as a proxy for your parents so that you can finally learn the lessons that you must integrate into your life before you can move on to healthier friendships and romances.

See "Chapter 3, Break those Chains" to learn more about freeing yourself from the memories and relationship styles that bind you to the past.

You don't have to live out a life filled with pain just because it started that way. You can be free of the past, and move on to more joyful relationships.

Detach with love

What if someone you love is caught up in an addiction? Ask yourself if he or she is addicted to one or more of these:

- Alcohol
- Drugs
- Sex
- Gambling
- Shopping
- Anger
- Lying
- Controlling
- Abuse (verbal, emotional, physical)
- "Poor me" self-pity parties
- Self-destruction
- Excess drama

When someone has a severe problem, you can get trapped in anxiously watching their struggle, and fearing for the worst. In addition, your sense of reality gets distorted and it becomes harder to maintain a healthy, positive outlook. Your energy is caught up in the tornado of the other person's destruction path.

Often, people fall so far into the relationship with a damaged soul that they take on the role of enabler. An enabler is defined as someone (usually well-meaning) who allows another person to continue their self-destructive behavior (such as substance abuse) by supplying excuses, helping out with finances, and/or helping that person avoid the consequences of their actions.

In essence, an enabler is a protector, and keeps the other person sheltered from the harsh reality of what they are doing to themselves.

You don't have to be a parent to be an enabler. Children coping with an alcoholic mother, for instance, will take on that role.

They do the housework, fix dinner, care for their siblings and bring mother another cold beer from the kitchen.

In their mistaken belief that their actions help their mother, the kids inadvertently keep her from hitting bottom. If she vomits, they clean her up and get her to bed, instead of allowing her to "come to" in her own mess on the floor, where she might get a cold awakening as to the extent of her problem.

Coddling an addict perpetuates the addiction

Enabling seems at first glance to be about loving the other person so much that you want to help them, but there are other factors at work and the situation can quickly become out of control.

If your teenager, for example, is on a self-destructive path of driving the car too fast without wearing a seat belt, and you keep bailing them out each time there is a traffic violation, then you have become their enabler. If you cover for them with a note to the school principal that they are home sick with the flu when truthfully they have a court appearance for reckless driving, you are an enabler.

You enable, or allow, the harmful behavior to continue without your teen having to face their actions and take responsibility. Each time you intervene, you cushion them from reality and allow them to continue being immature and irresponsible.

If you are around someone who drinks or uses drugs as a way to escape life, you can't help but be affected. All of the addictive behaviors listed above tend to draw us in and keep our thoughts centered on the addict.

But when you try to fix someone else's life, they resent you for it. The changes you might be able to convince them to do by threats and cajoling will not last because they are not coming from within that person, but from the outside: from <u>you</u>.

What about bribes? "I'll buy you a new car if you promise to drive more carefully!" ... "I'll take you to your favorite restaurant if you get your hair cut and cover up those tattoos."

Don't bribes work, at least for a while, to make life go more smoothly?

All statements that start "I will" and lead to "if you will then" are bribes. And they don't work in the long-term. You will find yourself having to escalate the bribe and the bling again and again, as you beg the other person to change.

They will make promises, but the addiction will not let them keep those promises. They are not thinking of you. They can't see past their pain to really notice you and your needs or desires.

What's going on? In reality, anyone with an addiction is trying to fill the hole of unhappiness that lives deep inside their spirit.

In order for you to be happy no matter what is going on in your life, you will need to practice detachment from the addict.

It doesn't mean you stop caring about them. What it does mean is that you will detach emotionally from watching everything they do. You will no longer try to control their actions. And you will stop rescuing them from the consequences when they get in trouble. It's called "tough love."

By allowing them to continue along the path they've chosen, you actually show them true love. You let them be in charge of their own life. When you slide away from the driver's seat and stop trying to steer for them, it is far more likely they will get a wake-up call and realize they need to change.

Is it love or infatuation?

There's a big difference between shallow love based on the excitement of physical attraction and the real deal.

Here are some ways you can tell if it's real. True romantic love is when...

- You are as supportive of the other person's life as you want them to be of yours.

- You readily forgive their mistakes instead of making a big deal over each tiny thing and holding a grudge.

- You want the best for them, and you encourage them to grow spiritually as well as emotionally without criticizing them for their flaws.

- You understand that the good of the relationship itself should be at the heart of every disagreement. You don't turn it into a win-lose battle where you do everything possible to get your way. You strive to forge a win-win outcome for the greater benefit of both of you.

- Your relationship is reciprocal in these three vital areas: love, trust and respect. If any one of the three is missing, you don't have a truly healthy relationship.

- You live each day with the intention of loving this person and being happy together, without trying to run their life. Making that decision and sticking to it on a daily basis will help turn around a relationship that's gotten off-track.

- You make a commitment to grow love (instead of sabotage it) and because of this shared goal, you bring out the best in each other instead of the worst.

These same guideposts can be used when you are deciding if a friendship is valid and is based on the strong principles of love and affection, or if it's codependent and imbalanced.

Love is a boomerang

When you put love "out there" in the universe, it will always come back to you.

Here's the caveat to understand, however, and it may save you heartache – just because you pour an abundance of love on a certain person does not guarantee that individual will love you in return, in the exact way you want them to love you.

Misunderstanding that principle is why unrequited love can lead to such bitterness and sorrow.

You will get love back. That's guaranteed. But not necessarily from the same source you directed your love toward.

So keep your awareness keen, and notice when others do loving things for you. Don't expect to get a particular type of love in return, such as romantic love, or you may overlook the special friendship awaiting you.

What are some of the kinds of love you might find if you open your heart?

The Greeks were smart about having different words in their vocabulary to define various types of love. Here are places you can find love in your life whether you call it affection, caring, liking, honoring, protecting... or "love":

- Your brothers, sisters and cousins.
- Your parents, grandparents, aunts and uncles.
- Children and young people.

- Love of God.

- Spiritual love for humankind.

- Romantic love.

- Friends, neighbors, teachers.

- Companion animals.

Chapter 18 – Summary: Get in the <u>love habit!</u>

The trick to the happiness power principle of Love is to not overthink it.

Just start loving people. Greet strangers with a smile. Ask the store clerks how their day is going. Pour affection and caring on everyone you meet.

And do the same for the man or woman in the mirror. Don't wait to love yourself. Start doing it today, right this minute. If it feels awkward, push yourself to do it anyway. It's good for you.

You'll come to a turning point in your life where you realize that you do love yourself just the way you are and you love everyone else, too.

Love makes the world go around – hop on and enjoy the ride.

Love somebody.

C
A
S
T
L
Enjoy
S

Chapter 19

E = Enjoy

Imagine that when you were born, you arrived with a limited lifetime warranty. Your physical body is guaranteed to last your entire life, however many days or years that turns out to be.

An important thing to remember about your life is that it does not come with any guarantees at all that you will <u>enjoy</u> it.

How much or how little you enjoy and cherish your journey on Earth is totally up to you.

What keeps you from enjoying life to the utmost?

Most responses to that question fall into the following categories:

- Too many problems.
- Disappointment.
- Heartache.
- Loneliness.
- Frustration.

- Fear.
- Pain.
- Anger.
- Sadness.
- Grief.
- Financial worries.
- Addictions.
- Illness in self and loved ones.
- Global strife.
- Overwhelming feelings of anxiety.
- Personal safety.
- Regrets.

Your life

Your mind, spirit and body comprise an integrated system. In order to be happy and feel satisfied, humans must learn to juggle five sometimes conflicting modalities: Physical, mental, emotional, spiritual … and archival.

Archival? What's that? The word might surprise you since it is not commonly referred to. I believe I am the first to do so in this context, and I feel it is an important one.

Imagine a desk chair with four wheels: that chair can tip over if more pressure (stress) is applied to one side. However, if you add a "fifth" wheel, you now have stability.

The addition of archival to the human picture means we add in the total history of mankind, the archives of humanity, to help the individual live more fully today.

In your own life, archival is related to your entire past, all the events, thoughts and actions that have brought you to this moment today.

How can these five modalities help you toward happiness? Let's take a look at them, one by one:

1. Physical: Take care of your physical needs, in moderation. The goal is healthy balance.

2. Mental: Rational thinking.

3. Emotional: Wellbeing.

4. Spiritual: We are all spiritual beings with an essence that continues after physical death.

5. Archival: Become a student of humanity. Historically, how do people deal with problems, grief and stress? Reconnect with your cultural background, the religion of your family, or search out something that is more meaningful to you if the old connections lack a vital ingredient.

The goal is peace of mind while being a useful addition to the planet.

Enjoy life through your senses

The average person is born with five senses: sight, touch, hearing, smell and taste.

If you are feeling stressed and unhappy, a quick remedy is to indulge your senses – pamper yourself for an hour. Scoop up all the daily miracles that your physical life provides and that you probably take for granted.

How often do you rush through a meal because you're in a hurry to get somewhere or do something else? You barely taste your food.

Today, slow down. Savor your meal... Savor your life.

Your senses are the gateway to feeling more centered in your life. Just because we are born alone and die alone does not mean we have to exist alone or feel disconnected from others.

Invite someone to join you on these sensory adventures. If you want to fit them into your own schedule, then a few minutes a day is all that's needed. These examples are intended to inspire you to see out sensory adventures of your own devising as well.

Sense of sight

- Go to a museum and enjoy the beauty of paintings and sculptures.

- Take a walk and pay attention to nature in the trees, flowers, butterflies and animals.

- When you're looking at someone, pause and really "look" – too often, we're busy with our thoughts while someone talks to us and we don't pay attention to all the visual clues and body language they give us. Notice the color of their eyes.

- Enjoy your gift of sight as you go about each day.

Sense of touch

- Take yourself on a sensory trip to the local grocery store and handle the produce. Fuzzy kiwi, smooth apple, rough potato, bumpy cantaloupe.

- Select a few items for the experiments below with smell and taste.

Resist temptation

The temptations of life's glitter and glamour can be alluring. If indulged in to excess, they can easily distract you from the crucial tasks and lessons that you are here to accomplish during your lifetime.

Seductive thinking lures you into turning your back on spiritual growth, while you stand with your legs firmly planted in material pursuits, momentary distractions and physical pleasures.

Meanwhile, your heart and soul are dissatisfied, and the void within grows deeper and larger. It becomes a dark abyss. The result is an unhappy life.

That void or "hole" is what people try to fill by eating too much, shopping too much, drinking too much, smoking too much, gambling too much. All the excesses are a vain attempt to feel better and more complete by filling the abyss inside.

You may have been trapped in an addiction and are now in recovery from it, or you may know someone who is addicted to, for example, spending recklessly to get a momentary rush. The thrill never lasts, and the addict is left with regrets and shame. To blot out those anxious feelings, they seek another rush, and the cycle continues.

The only way to break the cycle is to fill that hole inside. Here's how:

- Make time to enjoy your life and your time on this planet.

- Get centered with a core of joy inside that doesn't go away no matter what happens to you and around you. Most people find the joy by connecting to their spiritual higher self and a God of their understanding.

- Find happiness in the "small stuff" that makes up the average day in your life.

Technical assistance

If your life came with an instruction manual, there'd be a section in the back with tips on what to do if you need help. Since we are reaching the back of this book, here they are:

- If you have questions and concerns, don't isolate in your problem. Reach out to a friend or neighbor, or get professional assistance. The hotline to God can be found in the process of prayer and meditation.

- If you're not getting the exact results you want for yourself or loved ones despite sacrifice, prayer and a lot of hard wishes, try letting go of the specific outcome you want. Instead, focus on the experience you are having at this stage of your journey. Do all you can to your best effort without thought of certain rewards. Offer encouragement and support to friends without specifying a desired outcome. See how this shift in thinking makes your life a happier one.

- Abandon your resentment against the universe that things have not turned out the way you thought would be the "right way." Collect all your resentful feelings about disasters and crises that have befallen you and the people you care about. Now include the bitter thoughts that run along these lines: "What would it have hurt in the scheme of things for him to not be hurt so badly in that accident... for her baby to be born normal... for his cancer to go in remission... for her to get that much-needed job." Gather all these thoughts and shove them into an imaginary box. Tie it with ribbons or twine. Attach balloons and visualize the box floating off into the sky and out of sight. Realize that you had no power over the outcome anyway. The stress of holding onto those reins as if you could force things to go your way was pointless. Even though you had the best intentions for helping others, trying to control their lives has kept you unhappy and tense.

Chapter 19 – Summary: Troubleshoot common problems that keep you unhappy

Before you scream in frustration that your life is not going right, try these simple steps toward feeling happier and enjoying your life:

1. Did you eat today? The human body needs proper fuel and water. Don't forget your vitamins.

2. How is your general health? Do you need to take better care of yourself, starting right now? Get the help that you need and make a start on it today. You deserve to treat yourself with kindness and concern.

3. Is the problem a new one, or a repeat of an old one in a new guise? Pay attention to lessons that crop up again and again because that indicates you have not learned what they are trying to teach you.

4. Plan "me time" for each day. Start off in small increments until you get used to incorporating time for yourself. Set aside 3 minutes when you get up in the morning to focus on the beauty of the new day which you have not yet spent.

5. Reminder: the day will not be refunded if you spend it unwisely, but if you spend it well, it will enrich you with joyful memories and meaningful movement forward on your life path. Create your own joy, now that you know the shortcuts. Affirm that you exist "in joy" every single day.

C
A
S
T
L
E
Serve

Chapter 20

S = Serve

There are many ways to be of service to your family, business and community as well as the world at large via international charity efforts and goodwill events.

Please don't equate service with drudgery, because it's not. Or at least, it shouldn't be and needn't be.

Helping others

"Serve" is the seventh happiness power, and it's your instant cure-all for a lot of emotional ailments, including these:

- Loneliness.
- Low self-esteem.
- Discouragement.
- Shaky self-confidence.
- Shyness.
- Feelings of inferiority.

- Nervousness.
- Isolation.
- Feelings of unworthiness.

You <u>can</u> make a difference by reaching out to others. Seek out those who are less fortunate than you and do what you can to help them.

Inspire others at no financial cost to yourself, with a cheerful smile, with a kind word, with service work and with lobbying for better education, health care and other benefits.

Involve your heart in what you do. Reach out to help other people in your life. It doesn't mean you become an enabler or try to take control of someone else's life.

The good type of serving others is to benefit them in some way, even if only by smiling and wishing them a happy day.

If you want to point out an action they might take, avoid judging or controlling words. Invite them to evaluate how things are working for them now and to consider taking a different approach. Then leave it up to them whether they follow your suggestions or not.

In that way, you spread a positive message of healing and growth without becoming a puppet master.

When you get involved with volunteer work and other ways of helping others, that old feeling that you don't matter to anyone will dissolve.

You <u>do</u> matter! You are part of the human race, and we are by nature social animals. We need each other, and we need <u>your</u> contribution of yourself, your talents and your time.

Don't forget that helping others includes being a good listener at home and offering warmth and affection to your loved ones.

Practice being a good friend. Take time to make connections with the people in your inner circle that go deeper than casual daily interactions.

Get to know the people around you – what they enjoy, what they think and dream about. You may be surprised to uncover subtleties to the relationships that you've ignored all this time. And you both will be emotionally and spiritually richer.

Loving-kindness

At the heart of being of service to others is doing acts of random kindness or "loving-kindness." These are selfless acts to help someone else or an animal, or to cheer someone up with no thought of tangible reward.

You do it because it feels good to be nice!

"No act of kindness, no matter how small, is ever wasted."
~ Aesop (620 BC – 560 BC), in Aesop's Fable "The Lion and the Mouse."

Here's a secret way to build your own store of good feelings inside, to keep as insurance for days when you feel a bit low. Seek ways that you can do small favors for people, even strangers, without drawing attention to yourself or getting praise and recognition for it.

Other examples that may inspire you to get started on a life of service:

- At the grocery store parking lot, move that abandoned shopping cart out of the parking space next to yours so a car can pull in without hitting it. And be sure to put your own cart back at the store entry or in the space allotted for it.

- If you see litter on your neighbor's porch or lawn, pick it up and throw it away.

- When you pass an expired parking meter with a car parked at it, put a coin in the meter to add a few minutes' grace for the owner to return.

- Give someone your seat on the crowded subway or bus.

- Let another driver go ahead of you in traffic.

- At your fast food stop, buy an extra coffee and sandwich to give a street person.

- Join a group that knits, sews or crochets for people in need and shelter animals.

- Volunteer at your local mission or shelter to serve food or help in other ways.

The basis of your happiness

I believe that the highest good is helping others.

You will quickly find that, along with love, service to others can be the strong base from which you build a richly satisfying life.

When you give without expecting anything in return, something interesting happens. All of a sudden, when you least expect any reward, you'll be overwhelmed with all the goodness and benevolence that rushes back to you like a shower of gold.

You are not meant to live in isolation. If humans were meant to live alone, there are plenty of planets in the universe for each individual to be assigned a solitary home to live out their days in a special spacesuit.

We have developed extremely complex language systems that we would not have if we were not meant to socialize with our fellows and communicate thoughts, ideas and feelings.

If all we were intended to do is co-exist in a village, sharing communal food and shelter from the rain, wind and snow, then we would not need to speak. Crude pointing and grunting is not even needed by coyotes or wolves, and they survive fine in a pack.

We are not in a pack in the old sense, but rather in a new sense... a human PACT.

By getting out of yourself and helping others, you will gain perspective on your own life and find it much easier to let go of the small annoyances that happen to everyone.

You learn how to take things in stride more readily when you see the burdens that other people bear with little complaint.

The counterpart of helping others is to learn to ask for help yourself and become part of the process from both sides. This leads to humility, a valuable trait to cultivate during your happiness journey.

Bonus tip

If you feel discouraged and ineffectual... if you feel that you don't make any difference because you are not a huge success financially or otherwise in your life or career... if you feel there's no point to your life... then service work will fill your heart.

Here are more ideas for how you can be of service in your community:

- Read to the blind.

- Visit the housebound.

- Help adults learn how to read as part of a literacy program.

- Participate in a pet adoption event.

- Collect pantry items for a food drive.

- Recycle your cans, bottles, paper and plastic.

- Donate gently used household goods and clothing to a local charity.

- Support the arts in your schools by attending events and sponsoring the programs.

- Contribute your time and energy to conservation efforts. Clean up litter or plant trees at your neighborhood park. Help clean up the beaches and shores marred by trash and sludge.

A moral compass

When you focus on helping others, it's as if you have a new "true north" compass point that you can follow. Use it to guide your actions.

With this imaginary compass, spend a few moments of quiet time and ask yourself each day, "What can I do now that will have a positive impact on the lives of people near and dear to me? How can I make a real difference to others by being here at this time in Earth's history?"

Your new compass will help you avoid dramas about your own woes, because you'll be able to handle your own ups and downs more readily and take challenges in stride.

Work with others. Seniors, children, homeless, the needy, mentally and physically challenged people all can use your acts of loving-kindness in their lives.

Those who might seem at a glance to have nothing to offer in return, such as those hopelessly incapacitated by birth defects, accidents or severe disease, actually are in full service to humanity because they offer us opportunities to love them unconditionally.

For every pain you see, there are solutions available but you must be the one willing to reach out and help. Take an action towards the light.

When you love one person, you are linked into the power of universal love. Keep adding to the links in your life. Together, we can change this world to be a more loving and connected place. One day... war will come to an end.

Service to others will become a deep comfort to you, as it leads you to discover all your best qualities. You will be acting from a motive of unselfishness that creates a warm glow, because you've tapped the bottomless well of love.

And that "well" is the source of all the world's happiness.

Social reform, in addition, uplifts all of mankind and sets righteous goals to strive toward.

Create huge objectives for yourself in your life. It is not useless to start on a task that might appear daunting to the timid. Be brave. You cannot reach a goal at all without taking that first step toward it, no matter how small a beginning you make.

To serve is not to be a servant in a debased way.

Serving does not mean that some people are meant to be the masters and others the slaves. Such episodes in our world history are marks of evil. Even otherwise good people were led astray by wrong thinking that was disguised as "truth" or defined as a necessary evil. Necessary for whom? For the ones who profited.

Be a happiness magnet

If you stand in one place waiting for others to come and make you feel better, it will probably be a long wait. That behavior belongs to a toddler with a boo-boo.

You'll attract the wrong kind of people anyway, because you're more likely to draw in unhappy people who expect to complain about life with you, instead of looking for solutions together.

The cure? Seek out someone who could use a friend. Be a good friend to others. Spread happiness and cheerfulness wherever you go. There's enough doom and gloom out there already, so don't add more to it.

You can do more good with a sunny smile than a frown, and it's easily proven by testing it the next time you see another person.

To learn how to help people and be of service in a selfless way, seek out people who are already doing this and learn from them. You'll find them readily at volunteer groups. Remember you may also find complainers there, so pick your associates with care.

Notice those who are happy and befriend them. Observe their behavior and attitude. Imitate the way they approach others. Learn to reach out a hand of friendship to those still standing in the doorway as you used to do.

Chapter 20 – Summary: Give without expectations

When you do favors for others, or offer your assistance, strive to let go of the thought of what you might get from them in return. Don't attach strings to the gift.

Open your heart, freely love your fellow humans and wish the best for them without seeking what's in it for you.

If you are in business, give great value for the price you charge so that you are pouring more abundance "out there" than you are taking in.

The more you practice selfless giving and generosity of spirit, the more you broaden your own soul's ability to love and be loved.

When you are helpful only because you know the other person will help you, there's a stinginess factor involved. You end up meting out your time and favors, not wanting to give "too much" unless you are confident of recompense in like measure.

It's far better to give away more than others do. It will come back to you, maybe not from that same person, but the universal law of love shows that when you put love "out there" it comes back in full to the person who gave it.

When you follow the 7 Powers of Happiness, you will enjoy true happiness in greater abundance than you ever imagined.

Parting Words

My intention with this book – "GET HAPPY TODAY: Your Path to Lifelong Happiness" – is to share with you the process and techniques that I've learned and developed which allow me to be a happy person no matter what's going on in my life, even when my cash flow fluctuates, bad things happen and sad times arise.

As you shift your happiness mentality and make stronger choices each day, you will enjoy your life more. Be in joy! And your positive energy will radiate to everyone in your circle and beyond.

Please leave your comments at my Facebook page "Be-Happier." The link is http://facebook.com/BeHappierNow I hope to see you there.

And in the meantime, remember to use your Action Steps and the 7 Powers of Happiness – Choose, Accept, Strive, Trust, Love, Enjoy and Serve – whenever you feel discouraged or confused.

Take good care of yourself. You deserve to be happy for the rest of your life!

* * *